The Murder of Stacey Mitchell and Other Stories

Mark Tasmon

Published by Trellis Publishing, 2021.

While every precaution has been taken in the preparation of this book, the publisher assumes no responsibility for errors or omissions, or for damages resulting from the use of the information contained herein.

THE MURDER OF STACEY MITCHELL AND OTHER STORIES

First edition. June 28, 2021.

Copyright © 2021 Mark Tasmon.

ISBN: 979-8223096337

Written by Mark Tasmon.

THE MURDER OF STACEY MITCHELL AND OTHER STORIES

MARK TASMON

STACEY MITCHELL

In 2006, two young women shocked the world with a brutal crime that seemed straight out of a torture porn movie.

Valerie Parashmuti and Jessica Stasinowsky were two lesbian women who fancied themselves as vampires. They had been living together for a year before they took in a troubled sixteen-year-old named Stacey Mitchell.

The attractive Stacey, however, caused a rift between the two lovers. A rift they decided to mend by killing the young girl in the warped belief that this would show how much they actually loved each other.

These are the events that led up to that fateful day in 2006.

Perth, Australia was the epitome of a quiet, suburban town. But like any other town, it had its own share of family squabbles.

Stacey came from East Dorset, England originally. She arrived in Perth, Australia when she was ten years old. She didn't like being away from her childhood friends in her native England and became rebellious over the next few years. This all came to a head when her father went away on a business trip to Japan. Stacey and her mother got into a fight so bad that the young girl ran away.

Packed up with nowhere to go, Stacey was referred to Valerie and Jessica by a mutual friend.

Stacey's friend warned her that the young lesbians were eccentric but harmless. They were into the goth subculture and thought of themselves as real vampires. They would slice into each other's arms and drink each other's blood.

Stacey arrived at the home and the lesbian duo seemed easy going enough. Also living at the house was a twenty-seven-year-old man named David Ross John Haynes who took care of the place for his father.

Valerie and Jessica were eighteen and nineteen years old respectively. Only a few years older than Stacey, they had all the freedom she desired.

They drank booze, did drugs and danced the night away.

But they were extremely possessive of one another.

Coming up with the idea of going to the beach, Stacey entered their living room dressed in a bikini.

Jessica immediately noticed how smitten Valerie was with Stacey's attractiveness. The young girl had a vivacious personality and a body to match.

"What was that all about?" Valerie asked Jessica when Stacey left the room.

"What?"

"I saw you checking her out."

"What are you talking about?" Jessica mocked surprise.

A bizarre plan was then hatched. The two women decided to prove their love to one another by killing Stacey.

Valerie declared herself a "vampire" at the age of ten. After she began cutting herself, she drank her own blood. This obsession with vampirism grew as she got older. She would consume the blood of both herself and of her friends that she could convince into doing the odd practice with her.

She had been physically abused by her father from the ages of three to sixteen. Her father would ultimately go to jail for beating up her mother and would have beaten her to death had Valerie not intervened. Enraged that his daughter would physically challenge him, her father held a pair of scissors to her throat. The violent Valerie, however,r knocked him over the head with a garden tool.

But it was her upbringing of daily beatings and sexual abuse that primed her for the violence that lay ahead.

Jessica's background wasn't all that different.

She was abused and became a 'cutter', taking a razor to her arms and legs just like Valerie although she didn't drink the blood. She would also burn herself with cigarettes. Her parents divorced when she was young so when she met Valerie, the two were drawn to each other like coiling serpents.

Putting their jealousies aside, the two lesbians worked themselves up into the mindset needed to kill Stacey. They remarked to each other how annoying they found the young sixteen-year-old to be. Stacey had talked about killing herself and the young lesbians couldn't understand why she complained so much because she came from a privileged background.

Unbeknownst to them, housemate David was eavesdropping on their conversation.

He initially believed that the women were joking but then realized that the mentally unstable pair were serious. David interrupted and tried to talk the women out of their sinister plan.

"No one should destroy your happiness," Valerie declared. "And you should kill anyone that does."

"Fine," David said. "Just don't kill her. Kill someone else."

"No," Valerie said. "We're going to kill Stacey. And you're going to help. You can hold her down and-"

"Stop, just stop-"

"No," Jessica said. "We're going to do it. And if you try to stop us we're going to fucking kill you too."

Browbeaten by the women, David was then told to go to his room and to "turn the music up if he didn't want to hear the screams."

The women then lured Stacey into the living room where she was invited to "party it up" with them. They supplied the teenager with whiskey and gave her some 'downers' in the form of sleeping pills.

The combination of whiskey and the pills made Stacey drowsy and then she went to lay down.

Seizing the opportunity, Valerie took a concrete block and smashed it over Stacey's head. The crack was so loud that David heard it above the music.

He yelled from his room that he needed to leave the house as he was having an anxiety attack. Jessica then handed him a black t-shirt to cover his eyes as she led him out of the house so he wouldn't see the bloodied Stacey writhing on the ground.

With David out of the home, the couple continued their attack.

Turning up the music, the two wannabe vampires played Bach's "St.John's Passion."

The melody fits their fantasy of two creatures of the night preying upon an innocent.

Stacey tried to run away but her weakened faculties wouldn't allow her to go very far before Valerie caught up with her. Slamming the concrete block on Stacey's head, again and again, the cement piece broke in half.

Which prompted laughter from the women.

Stacey bled profusely but was still alive, trying desperately to make her way to the back door.

Then Jessica got into the act.

Taking a dog chain, she straddled Stacey's back and strangled her to death, finishing the job.

The entire attack took almost forty-five minutes.

Inexplicably, the two women became sexually aroused by the violence and the blood.

Taking their cell phones, they posed above Stacey's body, like hunters showing off their kill. They rubbed Stacey's blood all over themselves and began to make out. Satiating their bloodlust, they called David home. The young man arrived at a house with walls and floors covered in blood.

"Clean that shit up," the women commanded.

The following morning, the lesbians realized that they did not have a plan to dispose of Stacey's body.

Valerie then took out a notepad and began making a list of what they would need.

"Garbage bags. Shovel. Lyme," Valerie wrote.

"A chainsaw," Jessica said. "And a wheelbarrow."

"Cement."

Dragging David along, the two then went to the hardware store and purchased all of those items again with no real idea in mind other then they wanted to turn Stacey's body into mulch.

Not wanting to get their hands dirty, the lesbian couple then coerced David into getting rid of the body on his own. The houseboy didn't know what to do or where to put the body so he placed Stacey into a wheely bin and rolled her out to the shed.

A few days later, neighbors began to complain about the smell.

Police were sent to the house and they arrested the lesbian couple along with David.

The two lesbians laughed throughout the court proceedings, exchanging glances at each other and giggling.

"You have each had more than a year in custody to reflect upon the evilness of your crime," Judge Peter Blaxell said. "Yet you still lack remorse and obviously place no value on the sanctity of human life. Even more appalling are your admissions to the effect that at the time of the murder you were each sexually excited by the violence of the event."

The trial was a circus of horror. The footage taken from the mobile phone horrified Stacey's parents.

Two minutes of the film was shown in court. The two lesbians pulled a blanket back from Stacey's semi-naked body as they laughed, mocking her British accent.

"I beat the fuck out of her with a rock," Valerie said.

Yet despite this lack of remorse, the women only received twenty-four years for their crime. David would receive two years for being an accessory.

The lesbian lovers were separated upon their incarceration. Amazingly, they continued to try and communicate with one another through an intermediary, none other than serial killer Catherine Birnie. Birnie would transcribe Jessica's words in order to send a letter to Valerie who was housed at another jail.

"Now that you are gone I cannot breath," Jessica wrote. "It's anybody's guess where we will be in 5 or even 50 years from now, but one thing I do know, my heart is and always will be yours and yours alone. Do you speak to the moon? I still speak to her nearly every night. The moon will carry your words to me if ever you want to send them. My heart is consumed with the regret of time lost and time never had. But as either friends or lovers my mind is my universe and all I see is you."

Stacey's family continues to grieve. They joined a support group for homicide victims to little avail.

"Sometimes it makes you feel guilty when you don't think about her," her father said. "Obviously, you never think that you are going to ever go through anything like this in your life and then - bang - it happens and it's just like a nightmare."

PSYCHO GIRL : THE TRUE STORY OF CATHERINE BIRNIE

9

JENA DICKENS

Catherine Margaret Harrison was born on May 23rd, 1951. Her partner, David John Birnie, was born on February 16th, 1951 and died on October 7th, 2015 by way of suicide. The duo was famously known throughout Australia as: The Killer Couple. They were from Perth, Australia and were found to have murdered four women ranging in age from 15 to 31 years old, over a span of about five weeks. Their fifth victim managed to escape through the bedroom window, while Catherine was distracted by a knock at the front door. The woman immediately ran and found help. The press referred to the heinous murders as the Moorhouse Murders. The victims were taken to Catherine and David's home located at 3 Moorhouse Street in Willagee, in Western Australia, a suburb of Perth.

Catherine was only two years old when her mother died in childbirth while giving birth to Catherine's younger brother. Her brother also died, two days later. Catherine's father, Harold, couldn't manage raising Catherine on his own at that time so she went to live with her maternal grandparents. When she was ten years old, Harold petitioned the court to receive custody of Catherine again, and he won. There always seemed to be a battle. Catherine's father didn't want her, but then wanted her, always back and forth. After Catherine was convicted of four counts of murder, it caused her father to suffer a nervous breakdown.

When Catherine was twelve years old she met a boy named David Birnie and they began dating two years later when they became teenagers. Both Catherine and David came from dysfunctional families. Their home life was chaotic and messy, literally as well as figuratively. David's mother was an alcoholic and his father was away at work the majority of the time. His father died in 1986 after battling a long illness. The house, as well as his mother, were messy and unkempt. She left her older children in charge of taking care of their younger siblings. She refused to do anything when it concerned the children and their welfare. Allegedly, David's mother would leave the refrigerator door open so that the children could eat throughout the day. David was the oldest of five children. David's school friends, as well as the local priest, deemed the family dysfunctional. The parents never prepared meals for their children, the house was always a mess, and the Priest, before marrying David's parents, said that he felt that their marriage would never lead to anything good. Little did he know how accurate his assumptions would be.

Catherine and David met through mutual friends shortly after David's family moved to the same Perth neighborhood as Catherine and her father. Catherine's father felt that David was trouble and a bad influence. Catherine had begun getting into a lot of trouble with the local police ever since the two of them met. Harold begged and pleaded with Catherine to stay away from David and stay out of trouble. Of course, this just brought the two closer. Whenever two kids are told not to do something, they go out of their way to blatantly disobey.

Even in adolescence David began exhibiting violent and perverse behavior. When David turned fifteen he dropped out of school and began working as jockey apprentice for Eric Parnham at the Ascot Race Course. While there, David would hurt the horses and also began his perverse career as an exhibitionist. David committed his first rape shortly after. By this point he had spent time in and out of jail for several charges ranging from misdemeanors to felonies. He built up a reputation around town as a sex and pornography addict.

Catherine was an accessory to a lot of crimes because of her involvement with David. They built up an extensive history of numerous charges including: breaking and entering, trespassing, unlawfully driving a motor vehicle, and theft. Catherine took the time, while in jail, to decide it was time to get away from David and start over. David had to serve a long jail sentence, while Catherine got off with probation. With the help of her parole officer, she found a job as a housekeeper working for the McLaughlin family. She ended up marrying the families' oldest son, Donald McLaughlin, on her twenty first birthday. They went on to have seven children. One of her children, however, was killed in a car accident while he was only an infant, leaving her with six of her children to take care of. Catherine was never really interested in motherhood though, and wasn't proud of her children and her family like another mother might be. She wasn't concerned about the children or keeping up with the house. Catherine was never truly happy. Her thoughts kept going back to her childhood love, David Birnie. The family that she had left never saw Catherine as a violent or evil person. Not unless she was around David.

Catherine finally reconnected with David Birnie after a thirteen year separation, four weeks after she gave birth to their seventh child. David had escaped from prison and the two of them had begun seeing each other. Catherine left her family and everything behind when David popped back into her life. They finally moved in together and Catherine had her last name changed to Birnie, although the couple never formally or legally got married. They moved into a white brick, two bedroom bungalow on Moorhouse Street. The house was unkempt, the property looked untended, and the house needed a fresh coat of paint. Catherine was completely dependent on

David, emotionally and physically. Catherine was easily controlled and manipulated by David, and she would do anything and everything to make him happy. She never wanted to disappoint him. David had an insatiable sexual appetite and was said to have sex up to six times a day. He also accrued an extensive pornography collection and his brother claimed he always had someone. He always had a woman around. David's brother, James, had ended up staying with Catherine and David for a short while. James had just recently been released from prison after serving time for his own sex related offenses. He stayed with the couple for about six months. His brother went on to describe the numbing spray that David would spray on his penis before he had sex with all of the different women.

David and Catherine had exhausted all of their options sexually and began looking for new ways to pleasure themselves. They had spoken about abduction and rape, but had not realized that it would be just a few short weeks before they turned their fantasies into a heinous and perverted reality. Being as emotionally dependent on David as she was, it was easy for David to talk her into his abduction and rape plans. Catherine could never tell him no. She felt that she couldn't survive without him and would do anything to keep him. Catherine was completely codependent and David always seemed to be in control. She wanted David to have all the pleasure and excitement that he wanted but knew that they had exhausted all efforts between just the two of them.

The abductions, rapes, and brutal murders began on October 6th, 1986. The couple didn't really care who their victims were, as long as they were female and alone. Twenty two year old Mary Neilson arrived at the Moorhouse Street residence to inquire about some tires that David had for sale. Mary was a student at the University of Western Australia where she was pursuing her degree in Psychology. Once inside the house, David took Mary by knife point and chained her to their bed and gagged her. Catherine stood in the room and watched as David raped the girl repeatedly. After the rape, the couple took Mary to Gleneagles National Park. David raped her one more time and then strangled her with a nylon cord and stabbed her through the heart. The couple then buried Mary in a shallow grave. Catherine looked on while David committed these violent acts, however, she did not yet participate.

The second murder took place on October 20th. The victim was fifteen year old, Susannah Candy. Susannah was a high school student attending Hollywood High School. She lived with her parents and had two brothers and one sister. Catherine and David Birnie had been driving around for several hours that night in search of their next victim. The couple finally found a girl walking along Stirling Highway, by herself, trying to hitch a ride. As soon as she got into David's car she had a knife to her throat and she was taken to the Birnies' home. While at the home, she was forced to write letters to her family explaining that she decided to run away. David repeatedly raped Susannah while she lay bound and gagged. Catherine had gotten into the bed with them and tried to strangle her with the nylon cord, but Susannah began fighting back. They forced sleeping pills down her throat, and once she passed out they successfully strangled her with the cord. The couple took Susannah to the State Park and buried her in a shallow grave, like their previous victims. This was the first time that Catherine took part in the murder. Catherine never showed any form of remorse over what she had done. When later asked why she contributed she said, "I wanted to see how strong I was within my inner self. I didn't feel a thing. It was like I expected. I was prepared to follow him to the end of the earth and do anything to see that his desires were satisfied. She was a female. Females hurt and destroy males."

On November 1st, the Killer Couple comes across their third victim, Noelene Patterson. Noelene was on her way home from work when her car ran out of gas. Noelene was a bar manager and had been working at Nedland's Golf Club that day. She was standing beside her car when David pulled up to her and offered his help. The thirty one year old got into David's car and was immediately met with a knife at her throat. She was taken to Moorhouse Street where she was bound and gagged, while being raped repeatedly. The original plan, like the others, was to kill the girl that same night. David had seemed to develop feelings for Noelene however. Catherine noticed the fondness that David had for the woman and became extremely jealous and increasingly upset. Noelene represented the type of person that Catherine could only wish to be and she absolutely despised her because of this. Catherine gave David an ultimatum at this point. She put the knife to her own chest and said, 'you either kill her tonight, or I will kill myself.' It was on the third night, after being given the ultimatum, that David gave Noelene several sleeping pills and then strangled her. She was then taken to the park and buried beside the other victims. Catherine admitted to taking pleasure in throwing sand in the victims face as David coldly buried her with no remorse.

Catherine and David's fourth victim, Denise Brown, suffered the same fate as the previous women who had the unfortunate experience of crossing paths with the Killer Couple. Denise Brown was twenty one years old, and was taken on November 5, 1986 while waiting at a bus stop. She was gagged and raped repeatedly before being put into the car and taken to Pine Plantation, where she was raped again while David waited for a blanket of darkness to fall. After it got dark he took her out and raped her again, while stabbing her in the neck. As David began burying her, thinking she was dead, Denise surprised the couple by sitting straight up in her grave. David struck her in the head twice with an axe as Catherine looked on in shock and amazement. David has said that he learned bodies would decompose at a faster rate if you stabbed them.

Detective Sergeant Paul Ferguson was the first to realize that he could be dealing with a serial killer, after the fourth woman was reported missing. Years later he recalled his experience while working on the case. He recalls how this case still haunts him and when asked why replied, "Because it was the most interesting and horrific I've had in my career," and "I have things tucked away back here that I pray to God I never pull out of the drawer." All of the missing women had come from relatively good homes and they never got into any real trouble. Their families found the phone calls and letters they received very suspicious.

The couples' fifth and final victim was seventeen year old Kate Moir. She was on her way home, after a night out with her friends, when she was abducted by the couple. The date of this final abduction was November 10th, 1986. Kate was the only one of their victims that was able to escape and run and find help. David had left the house for work that day. Catherine was home with Kate. She forced her to call her parents and tell them that she would be staying at a friend's house. When Catherine heard a knock at the door, she left Kate alone, untied, and went to see who was there. Kate took the opportunity to escape through the open window and ran half naked to the nearest store. She ran in crying and pleading for help. Kate was taken to the Palmyra police station and questioned. She was able to give the police a full description of Catherine and David, as well as inform the police of the couples' address. After their arrest, Catherine admitted to knowing Kate, but the couple said that the sexual acts were consensual and she was a willing participant. The police performed a search of the Birnie's home and found Kate's bag, as well as a pack of cigarettes that Kate had managed to hide in the ceiling in order to prove that she was there. After hours of questioning, Catherine and David finally admitted to the rape and murders of the four women and agreed to show the police where they had buried them. Three of the victims had been buried in Gleneagle State Forest and one on the Pine Plantation. The couple showed no emotion, whatsoever, as the police dug up the graves. David was the one who showed the police the locations of the women, except for one. Catherine insisted that she be the one to show them where Noelene was buried. She showed no regret, only anger. She spat on Noelene's grave and made her strong feelings of hate toward her very vocal to the detective. She explained to the police, in great detail, how much she despised Noelene Patterson. As they were leaving, David turned to Detective Katich and said chillingly, "What a pointless loss of young life." They showed absolutely no remorse for what they had done. This statement stuck with the detectives for years to follow. They couldn't believe how little the couple seemed to care or regret what they had been done. In some ways, however, they thought Catherine was relieved that it was finally over.

Catherine admitted to not caring about participating in the rapes and murders of the women, until they got to Denise Brown. "I think I must have come to a decision that sooner or later there had to be an end to the rampage. I had reached the stage when I didn't know what to do. I suppose I came to a decision that I was prepared to give her a chance." The brutal manner in which Denise was murdered seemed to hit Catherine hard. She witnessed David not only stab her repeatedly but strike her in the head with the axe. "Deep and dark in the back of my mind was yet another fear. I had a great fear that I would have to look at another killing like that of Denise Brown, the girl he murdered with the axe."

In response to Kate Moir's escape, due to Catherine's carelessness with her victim, she said, "I knew that it was a foregone conclusion that David would kill her, and probably do it that night. I was just fed up with the killings. I thought if something did not happen soon it would simply go on and on and never end."

Kate Moir survived the abduction and attacks of Australia's most infamous serial killers. Instead of remaining a victim, she chose to be a survivor. She also sought to seek reform for the way her government handled cases like hers.

"I want to see no parole for wilful murder. I want a reintroduction of wilful murder as a charge. I want truth in sentencing. I want no parole for sex offenders and child sex offenders. We have been softening our justice system for years."

Kate Moir is a married woman and mother of three children. She constantly fights for the changes and justice she deserves. The following are quotes that were made by Kate, again concerning Catherine's parole and the possibility of her release.

"I want the legacy that I leave to be that of a survivor and a hero, not a victim. But enough is enough."

"I want the Attorney General to change the law and stop reviewing Catherine Birnie's parole. She does not apply for it herself, it is automatically reviewed and every time it happens, it causes me incredible pain."

"Every time I hear that her parole is being reviewed, I relive the nightmare. It causes significant trauma because I relive it and it feels like it happened yesterday. My name was always protected because I was a minor at the time I was captured, but due to the internet, if anybody googles my name it is everywhere and linked to the Birnie killings."

The couple appeared in court on November 12th, 1986. This was just two days after their fifth victim had escaped and they were arrested. The court proceedings took place at Fremantle Magistrates Court. They both refused any kind of representation, no plea was entered, bail was refused, and they were remanded into custody. Catherine allegedly took photos and the couple also recorded video of their criminal acts. At trial, the police were in possession of the video evidence. On February 10, 1987 a crowd gathered outside of the courthouse. When they saw the couple being ushered in for trial they screamed and chanted, "Hang the Bastards!" The community was outraged over the news of the serial killings that took place and wanted David and Catherine to receive the maximum sentence. They even wanted to reinstate the death penalty for David and Catherine Birnie.

Bill Power, the court reporter, spoke about the proceedings and the manners in which the couple acted while in court. He said that it would be something that would always stick with him, he would never forget.

"There was nothing distinctive about David and Catherine when they first appeared in court to face multiple murder charges in the serial

killings which brought an end to the mystery of young women going missing off Perth streets."

"They were a rather nondescript, ordinary looking couple you might find running a petrol station in a country town. David was a weedy little man and Catherine his drab, slightly buxom wife with a very sour face. Both were accompanied by male police officers."

"If you have ever witnessed a wild cat go off, then try and imagine some hellcat in the confined spaces of a narrow staircase. Catherine Birnie fought against the guarding police officers and refused to allow any of them to touch her as she screamed and spat her words at them until she reached the dock and spotted her beloved, David. Only then did she calm down."

It had also been said previously, by some people in the community that the couple never looked like the type that could commit such violent acts. They looked like normal and ordinary people. But the secret horrors of what occurred in their home on Moorhouse Street would paint a very different image of the couple.

Trial Judge Justice Wallace said in trial, "Each of these horrible crimes were premeditated, planned, and carried out cruelly and relentlessly over a comparatively short period."

Right before Judge Wallace sentenced Catherine, he delivered the following message to her. He explained that he did not believe that even though she pled guilty, that she was truly sorry for what she had done. She had pled guilty and avoided a long trial, and spared the victims' families from having to relive over and over what happened to their loved ones, but she showed no remorse, no emotion, no sympathy for the crimes she had committed with David Birnie.

"You willingly joined in the selection of your unfortunate victims, carried them off at

knifepoint, and held them in captivity for the sole purpose of the sexual gratification of your partner in crime and then murdered them, lest you be identified, and then finally mutilated them. You personally extinguished the life of two of your victims and certainly participated in the death of the third. The only appropriate punishment is the sentence I intend to impose, strict life security in prison."

Remember, Catherine was completely devoted, obsessed, and brainwashed when it came to David. She would do anything and everything for him to make sure he was happy. This is the driving factor that David used to manipulate and control her. He needed an accomplice and she was more than willing, and he knew it. Catherine and David received four separate life sentences for the abduction, torture, rape, and murder of Mary Neilson, Susannah Candy, Noelene Patterson, and Denise Brown. Under sentencing laws, their case was brought up every three years automatically for parole. Kate began a crusade to ensure that the couple remained in prison. She grew a social media presence and page entitled, We Support Kate, as well as worked with the Empowerment Foundation in an attempt to build an online reform petition. Kate also received support from Catherine's son, Peter. He chose not to release his surname to the public, due to the physical and emotional abuse he has been forced to face in relation to his mother's crimes. He had suffered personal and professional ruin, as soon as people learned about his family history. He had been turned down for jobs, lost jobs he had, and even lost his fiancé because of his family background. Peter was only five years old when his mother was arrested. He saw his mother on television because of it shortly after her arrest. When speaking out on the abuse he faced, he recalled horrible stories of what happened to him, and his siblings, while growing up. He also stated that the mandatory parole hearings, every three years, prevented him from getting on with his life. Having to hear about his mother and relive the violence his mother was responsible for every few years, was an interruption to his life, and it made it harder to maintain a sense of normalcy within his career life and personal life. In an interview with the West Australian, Peter stated, "I want the parole board to hear I don't want her out. I don't want to see her out." He also said, "I have had baseball bats to the head, I have been jumped on and kicked at. I have been knocked out."

After pleading guilty and receiving their sentences, David was initially sent to maximum security Fremantle Prison, he was eventually moved into solitary confinement. He did not get along with the other prisoners and was constantly getting into fights. The inmates frequently and violently attacked David. A day before he was due in trial for the charge of rape of an inmate, David hung himself in his jail cell. His suicide occurred in 2009 at Casuarina Prison. Catherine's request to attend David's funeral was refused.

Catherine was sent to Bandyup Women's prison where she was eventually employed as the head librarian. While in prison, the couple exchanged over 2600 letters, but were denied any other form of contact. Catherine's mandatory parole hearings were finally revoked in 2009, and her papers were subsequently marked: 'never to be released.'

While many people are against Catherine Birnie ever getting parole, one man stands against this argument. Perth QC Tom Percy disagrees with the opinion of people that had been saying that some people just don't deserve a second chance. The following quotes by Percy outline his argument of Catherine not remaining in prison and the likelihood of her harming the community, as well as his stance of being in favor of Catherine's parole.

"She should not be kept in prison to satisfy society's thirst for revenge."

"She has been there thirty odd years and you would think it might be time for us to say she has done her time. She has done her statutory minimum prescribed by the court, which was in possession of all of the facts."

"I am not sure she could really be a threat to anyone anymore, and all my information from Bandyup Womens' Prison is that she is a little old granny that goes about her work in the library like a church mouse."

"This case just so happened to be one that caught the public attention, even though she was not the prime mover in it. David is now dead."

"What's the point of keeping her in there? Sadly, it looks like she will never get parole, but I think she probably deserves it."

Despite his argument and fight to get Catherine released from prison, she still remains behind bars. She has not requested any new parole hearings, herself, as of yet. Some people in the community had gone as far as to say that if she were to be released, then maybe Percy should allow her to live with him in his residence.

It was now January of 1987. A letter written by Catherine Birnie, while in prison, eventually surfaced. It was a letter she had written to her six children in an attempt to explain some of her actions that led to her being placed in prison and why she left them in the first place. The letter reads as followed:

"Dear kids, Hi! Mum here...the reason I changed my name to Birnie was so that you kids wouldn't be hurt by the newspapers and television people. I am not proud of what has been said about me, but I have to live with that and the memories. As to why this happened, I can only

hope that the doctors can help me to find out.....I never stopped loving any of you kids. Maybe I was wrong about leaving you but I thought you would be safer with your father."

Catherine's husband, Donald, claimed that he had still wanted her back. This was after trial and after he heard of the horrific acts she had committed with David. He stated, 'you can't stop loving someone after fifteen years of marriage.' Donald's mother stood firmly beside her son, saying that Catherine had been good and non-violent, until David cast his spell over her. Catherine's nephew, Leonard Nock, stood beside his aunt claiming, "All Aunt Cathy wanted was someone to lean on. She never had a mother. She is a very caring person. She and I are very close. I used to call her my mum. She was never the violent type, she never used to hit the kids. It is not the Cathy we used to know and love." In Catherine's letter she also persuaded the children to tell their father to divorce her. She said their father needed to move on and this was the way it needed to be done. She didn't hold out any hope for her eventual release and didn't want Donald to wait for her, because it was never going to happen. She also asked the children to get permission from Donald to write back to her, and maybe even one day go and visit her. The family put the entirety of the blame on David. They refused to admit to or believe that Catherine had anything to do with the violence. During their prison visits, the family also failed to even ask Catherine the question regarding her guilt or innocence. They didn't want to hear the answer, therefore, they never even asked the question.

Catherine Bernie was up for parole in 2013 and again in 2016. She was denied both years. She is once again up for review sometime in 2019. "Now barring any reason to keep her in, and revenge I don't consider enough of a reason. She should be released."-Percy

Despite Percy's statements, Catherine Birnie remains in prison to this very day, with little to no chance of parole. People, even to this day, wonder if the abductions, the perverse rape, and heinous murders would have continued long past the few weeks they had gotten away with it. If they had never been caught, would they have continued? Finally, were there other victims that they never confessed to? Other gravesites that have yet to be located? It is too late for David Birnie to tell anyone, but Catherine still has the chance to admit to any other wrongdoing she had done before her permanent home in prison forced her to keep distance between herself and her lover. I guess we will never know.

"I honestly believe that woman has never given those victims one ounce of consideration, both the dead victims and the families of the

victims...They [David and Catherine Birnie] were parasites who lived off of each other. The most evil people I have ever, ever come across."-Detective Paul Ferguson.

The DeFrancisco Sisters

THE MURDER OF STACEY MITCHELL AND OTHER STORIES

Kori Solomon

CHAPTER ONE

Regina and Margaret DeFrancisco are two sisters convicted of first degree murder.

On paper, the two sisters look like two girls you would see at a church social.

In school, both were good but not great students. Margaret was the pretty one. She would get all of the attention from the boys but return little interest.

Margaret was a student at Jones College Prep School, a selective public institution that is considered one of the top high schools in Illinois.

A little on the shy side, Margaret had a quick wit and sense of humor. Sweet-looking and pretty, she had avoided any kind of trouble throughout her young life. Her early photos suggest, however, that her subtle smirk was a couldn't contain the narcissism that was growing within.

"You would look at Margaret and see right through her," one of her neighbors said. "It was black, like was nothing there. She didn't seem like she had depth, like she had compassion."

Regina had a love for animals, particularly ponies. She rode horses and in her words, "never lost a show."

Regina was also the more extroverted of the two, wearing her emotions on her sleeve. She could mouth off and had a chip on her shoulder. She also had a thing for 'bad boys', seeing them as a reflection of herself.

"A lot of girls get turned on by the 'thug life'," forensic psychologist Marnie Clark said. "The DeFrancisco sisters definitely fit that mold. They were not out to play Mrs. Cleaver when they grew up. They were attracted to the gang lifestyle. They thought the drama was exciting."

The girls were raised by a single parent, Nora DeFrancisco. Nora raised the two sisters and their brother Joey in the Pilsen neighborhood of Chicago. Their father, Augie DeFrancisco was a small-time burglar and convicted drug dealer who had no involvement in the girl's childhood years. Their maternal grandfather, Gilbert Smith, was a former Chicago cop who was fired from the force in 1960 after admitting that he was "friendly with certain burglars."

Growing up in Pilsen, however, the girls could not avoid rubbing shoulders with gang members. They became enamored with gang culture, learning who fought against who and what the names of the gangs were. There were the Latin Counts, Kool Gang, Villa Lobos, Bishops, among many other offshoots. The girls knew what streets signified what gang members' territory and memorized their hand signals.

"Chicago is simply rife with gangs," Clark said. "It is inescapable, even to those in the more affluent communities. There is still a choice, however. For whatever reason, the DeFrancisco sisters were drawn to the 'thug life'. To a young person, it looks 'cool'.

They are the classic examples of young women who could not see the big picture and thought the thug life was something worth aspiring to."

The two sisters, with their striking brunette looks, could not help but come into the cross hairs of the local gang members. They began wearing dark lipstick and teasing their hair out. Margaret would get a tattoo on her belly. Regina would have the letter "R" tattooed on her leg as well as a drawing of a heart just above her breast. They would hang out on street corners and in front of the local liquor store, chatting up the neighborhood 'gangstas'.

"The changes in their make-up and dress signified the changes in their personality," Clark said. "They grew bored during their time at prep school. Even ashamed. They did not want to see themselves as nerds and hated that aspect of themselves. Starting in eighth grade, it was time to start rebelling. By the time they reached high-school, the thug life was part of their persona. Dark make-up. Tattoos. Hanging out with gang bangers. Alcohol and drugs. But most important, they wanted all the drama that came with that kind of life. Who is out to get who, who dissed who and who shot who became their modus operandi in life."

Grandfather Gilbert, however, had seen this all before as a Chicago cop. He feared that the girls, particularly Regina, would become ensnared by the street gang culture. He tried to obstruct this from happening and found Regina a job with a local periodontist. He figured if he kept the girl busy with school and work it would keep her away from the idiots on the street.

Regina, however, did not have the emotional maturity to see the light. She showed up late for her first couple of shifts then she was fired.

But she had started dating a man named Johnny Rivera, a known member of Chicago's notorious "Latin Kings" street gang. Rivera had a rap sheet as long as "War and Peace" as well as more aliases than a Russian spy

Regina would learn how to package and deal drugs at the foot of Johnny. She would watch him put the cocaine into plastic bags, measuring it out by the ounce. They would drive around town and Johnny would introduce her to his customers, watching as he conducted the deals. The secret handshakes and secret lingo all became apart of Regina's world.

Officially crossing over from innocent prep school girl to drug dealing girlfriend, Regina lived a double life. She did manage to get a part-time job doing data entry work for a local law firm and had enrolled in the local junior college (Harold Washington).

Margaret was getting into trouble as well. Her grades in high school were slipping as she would sneak out at night to be with friends. She would often come to school looking "disheveled" according to one teacher who thought she looked like a child whose parents were going through a divorce.

And there was trouble on the home front.

Neighbors would report hearing the girls fighting with their mother on a daily basis.. The two girls were out of control with no father figure to put them in line. Nora would berate Regina whenever she would act up in school or get arrested and the girls would yell back.

In private, Nora would refer to her daughters as "the bitches".

Things would come to a head when Regina would get arrested for selling cocaine to an undercover cop. A single mom already strapped for cash as she had to support three children on her own, Nora was livid as she paid Regina's bail.

"How are you going to pay me back?" .

"I don't know!"

"Do you know how much it costs to bail you out of jail!" Nora screamed. "You are going to pay me back. You're going to pay me back every penny!"

CHAPTER TWO

"She needs money," Margaret said, her voice full of concern.

"How much?" Oscar asked.

"One thousand dollars. Can you help us out, baby?"

That was the scene set for the twenty-two year old Oscar Velazquez in June of 2000 as he spoke to the sister of his current teenage crush, Regina DeFrancisco. He spotted Regina around the neighborhood of Pilsen and quickly fell for her dark Irish-Italian good looks. Showing off his brand new Z28 Camaro, he chatted up the girls before he asked Regina out for tacos. The two began going out but Regina didn't like him...at first. Then she realized that he had some money and was all too willing to spend it on her.

"Oscar wasn't the typical guy that Regina would go for," Clark said. "Regina liked the 'bad boy', the thug. Oscar wasn't in street gang culture. He had immigrated from Mexico and actually had a real job, earning his living the old fashioned way as a truck driver. If anything, Regina would see someone like him as a sucker, someone who she could use."

Still, Regina was what Oscar wanted. He persisted in calling her, asking when he could see her again.

"He's a creepy guy," Regina told her sister, Margaret as her cell phone rang. She looked at the caller ID. Yep, it was Oscar.

"But maybe you can get some money from him?"

"Here, you talk to him," Regina said handing the cell phone to Margaret. "Just make up some baloney that I'm in jail or something."

"What?"

"Get rid of him. Tell him I need bail money."

"Hello, Oscar?" Margaret answered the phone.

"Yeah," Oscar said. "Who is this?"

"It's Margaret," she said, sounding as if she was trying to stifle tears. "Regina is in jail. She's locked up."

"What?"

"They put her in jail for something she didn't even do. They want one thousand dollars. One thousand dollars to bail her out."

Margaret smiled like a devil at her sister.

"I can help," Oscar said.

"No," Margaret said, sniffling. "It's too much."

"It's for your sister."

Oscar would persist in his willingness to help out, however. Margaret played him like a violin, agreeing to meet with Oscar to take his hard earned money.

"Oscar gave Margaret the money in the hopes of scoring points with the sisters," Clark said. "He thought that by being 'nice' and bailing them out of trouble they would find him attractive. Instead, it just fueled their contempt for him. These girls liked thugs. Bums. They cared little for Oscar's chivalry."

Regina would not use the money to pay back her mother, however. She would give the money to her real boyfriend, Johnny, who bought an "old school ride" car with Oscar's money.

Oscar would call Regina over twenty-four times during the next five days wanting to know what happened. He began to feel like the sucker he was.

He had a wife and kids in Mexico. But here in Chicago he fell for the brown-haired beauty and became all too willing to be her patsy.

"Oscar was playing with fire," Clark said. "He just didn't realize how far gone the girls were in terms of narcissism. He didn't see the fact that they didn't even see him as a human being. All he saw was batting eyelashes and pretty faces. He was totally smitten with Regina despite the fact that he had a wife and kids back in Mexico. Here he was, in Chicago, where he was free from the responsibilities of family. He could have a little fun and if he had to spend some money to do it, so be it."

CHAPTER THREE

The two sisters were surprised at how easy it was to extract money out of Oscar. With one fake phone call, they had one thousand dollars cash to their name.

"They were both attractive girls in the neighborhood," Clark said. "They were young, looking up to gang members and drug dealers for the power they had. But the girls realized that they had their own power. The power of budding sexuality that could make men do what they wanted. They could trick men into doing things for them with a future promise of sex."

Oscar continued to call and it would be only a matter of time before he would be confronted with the truth that he had been lied to. The girls had to construct a plan to get rid of him.

"I have an idea," Margaret said, picking up the cell phone and calling their fifteen year old friend, Veronica Garcia.

"Need your help," Margaret said as Veronica picked up.

"For what?" Veronica asked.

"I need a gun. Can you get a gun?"

"A gun?"

"Can your boyfriend get a gun?"

Veronica, like the DeFrancisco sisters, was enamored with street gang members. She had a boyfriend who could obtain whatever you needed, drugs or guns.

"Why?"

"We're going to stick up and rob Oscar," she said.

"You're not going to kill him are you?"

"We're just going to scare him a little," Margaret laughed.

Veronica did as she was asked, getting a gun from her boyfriend and heading straight over to the DeFrancisco sister's home.

"Nice," Margaret said, looking the pistol over, closing one eye as she looked through the cross hairs. "So where we going to do this?"

"Right here," Regina said, waving her hands around the living room.

"No way," Margaret said. "If the neighbors complain about us screaming and yelling then they're going to hear a gunshot. Duh."

Regina looked around the home. The basement door caught her eye.

"We'll lead him down there," Regina said, leading her sister down the basement steps. "Nobody can hear anything down here. The noise will be drowned out."

"Here," Margaret said, removing some blue tarp from the shelf. She spread the material down on the basement floor in front of the steps. "We can't leave any blood stains."

"Check you out," Regina laughed. "Miss Perry Mason."

Margaret laughed as she flattened out the tarp, placing it in a perfect line with the basement stairs. "Okay," she said, walking halfway up the steps. "So if we shoot him from here," pointing her forefinger into a gun. "He'll fall straight down there."

"Perfect."

The two sisters giggled and gave each other fist bump.

"Here is where the disconnect took place," Clark said. "They had embraced an environment and a culture where there were a lot of faux tough guys. Guys who said they would commit violence but for the most part it was all talk. The girls took it literally. At no point did they realize the gravity of what they were doing. They wanted to be 'gangstas', they wanted to be seen as 'hard'. They didn't have the maturity or the experience to realize that all of those 'gangstas' that they look up to are in jail. They didn't see Oscar at all. He was less than human. Something that is used, discarded and desecrated when it is no longer of use."

CHAPTER FOUR

Oscar was surprised that Regina finally called him back.

"Hey," she said, her teenaged voice soft and inviting.

"You're out of jail?" he asked.

"Yeah," she said. "I really appreciate what you did for me. That was really sweet of you."

"No worries," he said. "I need my money back. Been calling you like crazy."

"I'm sorry, I've just been busy."

"Yeah, I understand. But I need my money back."

"I was wondering if there was some other way I can pay you back?" she said in a sensual tone of voice.

"Like?"

"Like, I know you think my sister is hot, right?"

"What's that got to do with anything?"

"It is something we've been thinking about," she said. "But if you're not cool with it, it's okay."

"Not cool with what?"

"We were wondering if," Regina giggled. "If you can come over for a threesome."

Oscar couldn't believe his luck. He had heard of white girls being freaky, he just didn't think he would ever be able to experience it himself.

Naive to their plan, he rushed over and parked his car outside their mother's home in the South Side of Chicago.

He knocked on the door and was greeted by Margaret and Veronica Garcia, a friend of the two sisters. He didn't see the .38 caliber semi-automatic pistol had in her back waistband.

"Does anyone else know you're coming over?" Margaret asked.

"No," Oscar mumbled, shrugging his shoulder.

Margaret nodded her head and let the young man in. He saw Regina step into the room holding a bin of dirty laundry.

An awkward silence ensued followed by even more awkward smiles. The two sisters fed off each others willingness to go through with the plan. Even if one of them had second thoughts, they would be deemed "soft" by the other.

They had to go through with the murder.

Both women looked over at the young man with come hither looks. Regina said nothing as she opened the basement door and walked down.

"You go with Regina," Margaret said smiling.

"Right," Oscar said, his heart pounding in anticipation as he followed her down.

Oscar heard Margaret's footsteps behind him. What he didn't know was that she had a gun pointed at the back of his head.

When he reached the bottom step, she pulled the trigger.

The young man died instantly, falling face first in the tarp.

"Holy shit!" Margaret said. "I had no idea it would be that fucking loud. It doesn't sound that loud on TV."

Margaret came down the stairs. She kicked Oscar in the head hard, sending more blood spraying across the floor and wall.

"Nobody heard," Regina said as she knelt down and began rifling through Oscar's pockets.

"What the fuck was that?" Veronica said, calling down from the top of the basement steps.

"Did you see that? " Margaret asked. "He fell down like a baby!"

The sisters took out his wallet which had over $600 cash. They took his cell phone then ripped off the sterling silver chain from his neck.

"What the fuck happened?" Veronica said, her voice trembling as she came down a few steps.

"We shot his ass," Margaret said. "He's dead. Look at that shit, he's bleeding through his ears."

"Why did you do it?" Veronica screamed. "Why? Oh my God!"

"Shut the fuck up!" Margaret screamed.

"Don't just stand there," Regina commanded. "Come and help."

Their lifelong friend could only watch as the two sisters took out his car keys and wrapped up his body in a flowery bed sheet.

CHAPTER FIVE

"The girls suffered from what I call the 'Lord of the Flies' syndrome," Clark said. "Here they are hanging out with drug dealers, obtaining guns, killing men in the basement. There is no parental figure in sight! They are left to fend for themselves and the end result is murder and mayhem."

With the dead body in the basement, both sisters peeked out their window, waiting for dark.

Confident that the entire neighborhood was asleep, they opened the door and carried Oscar's body out of the home.

The three girls struggled carrying the dead weight, wrapping his body with a comforter and the flowered bed sheet.

They opened up the trunk and placed the body inside.

"What are you guys doing?" a woman yelled from a window across the street.

The girls looked up startled.

"We're getting rid of some furniture" Regina called out. "No worries."

The girls waved at the neighbor as she moved away from the window.

"Nosy bitch," Regina whispered.

Margaret giggled. Veronica still scared, said nothing.

They got into the vehicle and drove to a vacant lot where they took out Oscar's body again.

"This is hard work," Regina complained. "Shit!"

They plopped the body on the ground, looking at it for a beat before Regina reached back into the trunk. She pulled out a bottle of nail polish remover and poured the liquid over the tarp.

"Are you sure that's gonna work?" Margaret asked.

"It says 'highly flammable'," Regina said, shrugging her shoulders.

Margaret lit a match and set the material on fire.

The flame went up immediately, the girls could feel the warmth on their faces in the cold Chicago night.

"Told you this shit would work!" Regina said.

Then as fast as the flame started, it quickly died down.

"Light another one," Regina said.

Margaret threw down another match, getting the flames going again as Regina doused the tarp with the remaining nail polish remover.

Satisfied, the girls quickly got back into the Camaro and drove off.

**

An anonymous call came into police headquarters reporting the fire in the vacant lot. The caller investigated further, however, and saw Oscar's arm sticking out through the fire. He called 911 again with a sense of urgency, telling them of the body.

CHAPTER SIX

When police on scene identified Oscar Velazquez' partially burned body, their initial knee-jerk reaction was that this was the work of a local street gang, a drug deal gone awry. But when they found the nail polish remover bottle, however, they quickly realized that this was the work of amateurs. A jealous girlfriend maybe.

Meanwhile, the DeFrancisco sisters cruised around town over the following days, trying to pawn off the Camaro.

"This is where the sisters make the guys in 'Dumb and Dumber' look like geniuses," Clark said. "They had only pre-planned the front end of the murder. Like most impulsive killers, they had no idea what to do after. Their greed took over and they decide to sell the Camaro. They have no papers for it, duh, and really can only sell a stolen vehicle to a thug. They find no takers as even the dumbest street gang member isn't going to buy a hot car from two teenaged girls. So they cruise around town and Oscar's brother spots them in the car."

The girls, failing in their sales efforts, would later abandon he vehicle behind a storefront and set it on fire.

**

The day after Oscar's killing, a mutual friend named Jessica Benitez stopped by the house. Jessica went downstairs and watched Margaret mop up a stain of blood near the basement steps.

"The hell is that?" she asked.

Margaret said nothing as she poured bleach over the blood, scrubbing hard.

"Dude bled all over the floor," Regina said. "But only after Margaret kicked him in the head. We called him over, told this idiot we'd have a threesome with him. Then we robbed his ass."

"But the blood stain on the floor-" Jessica asked, watching Margaret clean up.

"We killed a guy," Margaret said without remorse.

"He was going to kill us!" Regina said. "Margaret shot him in the back of the head. We searched his body and found a gun in his waistband. Then we wrapped him up in plastic and put him in his car."

"Holy shit, girl," Jessica.

"We're about to go on the run," Margaret announced.

"Aren't you scared?" Jessica asked, looking back down at the blood stain in the basement.

"I ain't scared of nothing," Margaret said. "You should have seen his head when I shot him. His brain oozed out like cheese."

Margaret made a rolling motion with her hands.

Jessica then accompanied Margaret to the store she purchased a bottle of blonde hair dye for her "disguise."

"We see here how the whole street gang culture has influenced the behavior of these girls," Clark said. "At any point in time, Veronica or Jessica could have went straight to the police. But they get caught up in the drama of the moment. The so-called 'loyalty' to their friend who, quite frankly, would shoot them up in a heartbeat if they knew that they were going to be a snitch."

Going off the tip from Oscar's brother, the police show up to question both Regina and Margaret. The duo denied ever seeing Oscar.

They then go to interview Veronica Garcia.

They found the jittery fifteen year old to be a different story, however. The teen quickly crumbled under the pressure of questioning and told the police the entire story.

Feeling the heat, the DeFrancisco sisters go on the run...

CHAPTER SEVEN

For all of their stupidity in committing the murder, the DeFrancisco sisters deftly avoided capture for almost two years.

They decided to split up. Margaret would go to live with their maternal aunt in Roscoe, Illinois, an hour and a half drive away from where they lived. Roscoe was a small town with less then 10,000 people, a far cry from the drug infested streets of Chicago. Margaret's worst dreams were now realized. She was now a nerd who had to stay inside all day long, living in a boring cul-de-sac with no street gang action. Neighbors would remark that they would never see her and if hey did she would quickly go back inside.

Living underground without detection, it took a broadcast of the television show AMERICA'S MOST WANTED to generate an anonymous tip which led to Margaret's whereabouts. Police staked out her aunt's apartment and entered, finding Margaret in her bedroom with a blank look on her face.

"My feelings were hurt bad because she (my wife) did something behind my back," Margaret's uncle by marriage said later. "I knew (police) were going to find her anyway."

Seven months later, Regina was captured in Dallas living with her Latin King boyfriend, Johnny Rivera.

Initially, she did not even know where the gang banger lived. She just knew the town, Laredo, and she journeyed there by bus. Regina would eventually find him, locating one of his relatives. She would live under an alias and claimed that she worked as a maid.

Police knew better. Regina made money by selling drugs under the Latin King banner.

Unlike Margaret, Regina had evaded the scrutiny of the America's Most Wanted viewers.

Her capture came about because she could not stop hanging out with the wrong crowd.

Two sheriffs were had mistakenly arrived at her boyfriend's apartment, wanting to serve a warrant to someone else.

Rivera allowed the deputies to enter his apartment but he had left a marijuana flake on his table. Police searched the apartment further and found several packages of crack cocaine ready to be sold.

The deputies arrested Rivera. They searched inside the apartment and interviewed Regina, who was groggy from a cocaine high. She showed them her false Texas identification and they let her go.

But the deputies smelled something fishy on her aside from marijuana. They had the apartment manager set up a meeting with her. She arrived at the complex in an SUV with another man. The police approached and the SUV sped away.

The high-speed chase down residential Dallas streets reached upwards of 90 mph. The SUV then slammed into a center median, the front tires blowing out.

Regina got out of the car and tried to sprint away. A deputy tackled her and they fell to the ground, her cell phone skidding across the gravel road. Sifting through her pockets, the officer found over $1,500 cash.

She was taken to Dallas County Jail where they discovered her true identity.

"We pulled her out of jail," said a Deputy Dodson. "I asked to see one of her tattoos, and she showed me...I called her by name, but she never said a word to me. She knew it was over."

She was then extradited to Illinois to stand trial for the murder of Oscar Velazquez.

CHAPTER EIGHT

The trial of the two women began in July of 2004 and both sisters pleaded not guilty by reason of self-defense.

But their friend, Veronica Garcia, had cut a deal with prosecutors in return for a lesser sentence. She would provide the testimony that would damn the two sisters to prison.

Garcia said that she didn't know what the sisters had planned. She had simply provided the gun to the DeFrancisco's which she thought would be used for a robbery only.

"I didn't see her shoot Oscar," Veronica said.

The prosecution brought forth additional witnesses in Jessica Benitez, Luciana Macias, and Maria Constantino, the neighbor.

"Both of them told me that they killed Oscar," Jessica said. "Margaret kicked him in the head so he could die faster."

"I saw them load the body into the back of the Camaro," Constantino said. "Regina told me that she planned out the killing."

Margaret, however, maintained their innocence. She said that Oscar came to the apartment angry because the sisters had tricked him out of one-thousand dollars.

"I shot him to protect Regina," Margaret said.

"Then why didn't you tell the reporting officer what happened?" the prosecution attorney asked.

"We would've got in trouble," Margaret said. "If I told the truth, I would've been there longer."

Regina DeFrancisco would also take the stand and claim self-defense as well.

"I came out of my bedroom," Regina said. "And he was there, cursing and screaming. He pulled a gun on me. I thought I was going to die. I curled up on the floor, in a fetal position. I begged for my life. Then I heard a gunshot and saw Margaret standing over Oscar, holding a gun."

"Whose idea was it to dispose of the body?"

"Veronica knew of this vacant lot," Regina said. "It was her idea."

The jury would deliberate for over six and a half hours. Regina would be found guilty of murder. Margaret's jury, however, was unable to convict her. There was and 11 to 1 deadlock with one juror believing that she should be acquitted. The juror did not believe that someone so young could commit murder.

Margaret was then released from custody and told to await retrial. She had a baby during this time, a girl, and would find work as a nursing assistant while she awaited another trial.

Four months later, Margaret would be given another day in court. Veronica Garcia would once again be the star witness for the prosecution, detailing the exact same testimony as before.

There would be no deadlock in this second go around as Margaret would be convicted of first-degree murder.

Regina would be sentenced to 35 years in prison while Margaret would be sentenced to 46 years. Both women are now jailed at the Dwight Correctional Center. They have each filed appeals which have been denied.

"The girls cared nothing about Oscar Velazquez," Clark said. "In the end, they remained true to their own narcissistic nature. They only cared about what was happening to the next. They cared about nothing about the now fatherless children Oscar Velazquez would leave behind nor about the fact that the took his life."

Veronica Garcia was jailed for five years. She served her full sentence and has since been released.

"This is a cautionary tale if there ever was one," Clark said. "The sisters had it all. They had access to one of the finest schools in their state. Yet they chose to throw it all away for short money and the cheap thrill of the 'thug life.' In the end, they got to see what the 'thug life' was really all about. Mindless violence where everyone is out for themselves, especially when there is a plea bargain to be made. They could have had it all had they stayed on the straight and narrow. Now they have nothing."

WITCH GIRL : THE TRUE STORY OF MARLENE OLIVE

PAM HAMILTON

Marlene Olive was the instigator in the double murder of her parents in 1975. The killings were referred to in the press as the barbecue murders as the sixteen-year-old Marlene and her twenty-year-old boyfriend disposed of her parent's bodies in a barbecue pit in a state park. Her boyfriend, Chuck Riley would be tried as an adult and sentenced to life imprisonment. Marlene would be tried as a juvenile and released at the age of twenty-one.

EARLY LIFE

The marriage of James and Naomi Olive started out happily enough. The couple had been married for fourteen years and were anxious for a child of their own. They both wanted a girl and found a newborn in Marlene.

Marlene was adopted a day after she was born. James would play the role of the doting father while Naomi would adopt a "very clinical approach to motherhood" according to friends. James had lost his life savings in a failed business project but remained optimistic about the future of his family. He found work with an oil company and was forced to travel abroad. He liked the travel and discovering new places but his wife hated it. She would become an alcoholic shut-in and often accuse James of having affairs which would prove to be non-existent.

"The stage was set for disaster," forensic psychologist Paula Orange said. "Jim Olive was the eternal optimist, always seeing the good in circumstances that looked doomed to failure. And with a schizoid wife in tow, the odds were against him. What would happen in their lives is a classic example of nature versus nurture. Marlene was nurtured by an abusive schizophrenic. How would her life have turned out differently if she had been adopted by a different couple?"

A PARANOID MOTHER

By the time Marlene was five years old, her adopted mother was diagnosed with "schizoid personality with paranoid features." One acquaintance said of their relationship, "she (Naomi) either smothered Marlene or ignored her."

Still, despite the affection she lacked from her mother, she had relatively happy early years as Jim settled his family into the country of Ecuador. But when Marlene was ten years old, she discovered some paperwork in her father's desk.

She found out she had been adopted.

"The story goes that Marlene was playing in her father's den when she discovered the papers," Orange said. "I don't know if I believe that. Marlene was very, very smart. At the age of ten, she probably deduced that the Olives were not her biological parents and began snooping around."

The Olives had no choice to admit the truth when Marlene showed the papers to them. But they did lie to Marlene by telling her that her biological mother had died in a car accident shortly after giving birth. With the truth now in the open, Marlene's relationship with her adopted mother began to deteriorate. The relationship regressed from simply ignoring each other to all-out hatred.

"Marlene became very angry at her parents, particularly her mother," Orange said. "She felt as if she had been bought. She felt alienated from the world at large and this revelation only increased her hatred for her adopted mother. Before she knew of her adoption, Marlene may have held some animosity in reserve as she would have gotten attached to her adopted mother as if she were her biological parent. But now that she knew that there was no blood relation, all gloves were off. Marlene could give into her hatred."

Now, at only ten years of age, Marlene entered a state of confusion. She didn't understand how she could have an adoptive mother which she called "mom" and a biological mother which was her "mom" as well. She began to brood over her "real mom" and wonder about her identity. Ultimately, Marlene would never meet her biological parents (her birth mother was a wealthy Virginia teenager who had a fling with a Scandinavian sailor on leave from his ship).

RETURNING TO THE USA

In 1973, Jim's oil business ventures brought him to the San Francisco Bay Area and the family settled in San Rafael. But their arrival back in the USA was greeted with a decrease in Naomi's mental health. She became even more of a recluse, refusing to leave the home while holding multiple conversations with "voices in her head."

Marlene did not like the Bay Area much at first either. She had spent the majority of her life in Ecuador and was more comfortable speaking Spanish than English. Marlene had been a bit overweight in Ecuador and was forced to attend strict private schools. When she returned to the United States, she was released from the boring school uniforms and realized that she could attract the opposite sex as she began to lose weight.

"It didn't take long for Marlene to go into a rebellion," Orange said. "She had the shock of discovering that she was adopted and then had to deal with the culture shock of moving to the San Francisco Bay Area. She developed ulcers and was given tranquilizers."

Marlene retreated into her own world. She would spend her nights watching horror movies indulging in her obsession for the macabre as well listening to a "glitter" rock performers like David Bowie. She would mimic his dress with platform shoes, tight jeans and she would put sparkle make-up on her face.

As Marlene entered her teenage years, her mother's behavior not only got worse but embarrassed her in front of her peers. Marlene would have friends over the house and

Naomi would interrupt their conversation with inappropriate statements.

"Don't pay any attention to her," Marlene would tell her friends. "She's a drunk."

Their arguments then became more hurtful. Naomi would call her adopted daughter a "guttersnipe," a "no good swine", and that she was the daughter of a "whore".

"The mother was schizophrenic," Marlene's attorney Terrence Hallinan recalled. "She used to beat the daughter pretty seriously."

Naomi always kept the curtains closed, as if trying to keep the world out. She spent a lot of time in bed and obsessing over her tropical fish. She was also gaining weight and became jealous of her daughter who was blossoming into a beautiful young woman.

"She started having some pretty serious conflicts with her mother," Orange said. "But, of course, most teenage girls start to have conflicts with their mother during that season of life. Marlene got along fairly well her father but her mother was a whole different kind of strange. On one occasion, her mother took off all her clothes and began dancing around the house, touching her genitals. She would taunt Marlene and say 'this is what your mother was really like. She was a whore. You'll be one too.'"

The labeling of Marlene as a whore became a recurring theme throughout the conflicts between Marlene and her adopted mother. Naomi kept needling Marlene with the

accusation that her birth mother was promiscuous and that
Marlene would end up the same way.

"Marlene actually began visualizing herself as a
prostitute," Orange said. "Because of what her adopted
mother said about her biological mother, Marlene actually
began to believe she was destined for the same fate and it
turned into a self-fulfilling prophecy."

"She (Marlene) was constantly fighting with the mother,"
Hallinan recalled.

Marlene would fight back, often calling her mother a
"bitch" and a "crazy lady who lays around like a pig drinking
all day."

The fights would frustrate Marlene to the extent that
she would bite on her arms, developing layers of scar tissue
over time. These arguments would often end with Marlene
locking herself inside the bathroom with Naomi pounding
on the door to force her to come out.

Marlene knew that her father adored her. He would
arrive home from work and be the peacemaker between the
two. He would achieve a stalemate which would never last
too long.

By the time Marlene reached high school, her abusive
home life would spill over into her schoolwork. In freshman
year she was arrested for shoplifting and released to her father
after a talking to by the police. She began receiving poor
grades and took pills for her "nerves".

She also began dabbling in the occult and started to date
a self-professed "warlock". The teenaged boy introduced

Marlene to witchcraft and weed as well as sex. Naomi took pleasure in discovering the young Marlene being deflowered in her home.

"Naomi was probably the first mother in history to take a sick pleasure in having her daughter lose her virginity," Orange said. "Naomi took it as a validation of her own prophecy about Marlene, that she would become a hooker."

BOYFRIENDS AS TOOLS

Things didn't last long with Marlene's first boyfriend. Her "warlock" dumped her as he didn't want "anyone clinging to him." Marlene became an emotional wreck and began writing poetry in order to express her thoughts.

"no one stops

to step into my life

and those in it have long ago

fallen asleep.

I have been empty for so long."

With her heart broken and her mother's continuous verbal assaults, Marlene began looking for a way out. A tool that she could wield to eliminate her mother.

She saw that tool in Chuck Riley.

Charles Riley, better known as "Chuck," was an overweight, awkward teenage boy who weighed over 340 pounds by the age of sixteen. His father was a bakery worker and his mother was a nurse's aide. He dropped out of high school in his senior year, finding work as a newspaper and pizza delivery driver.

His life achievements were owning a Hot Rod car and shooting guns but was unpopular in school and in the community until he became a small-time drug dealer. The irony was that in selling marijuana, he became popular and he stuck with that as a career path.

As Riley's confidence grew, he targeted the slim, green-eyed Marlene. She accepted a date with the overweight Riley and the two began dating.

"Chuck Riley was an overweight shy guy with very few friends," Orange said. "So when Marlene not only pays attention to him but agrees to be his girlfriend, he is just head over heels in love and can't believe his luck. He basically becomes her lap dog, he will do anything she says as he doesn't want to lose her."

Riley wanted to impress and keep Marlene so badly that he began making improvements in himself. He began slimming down in weight and changing his wardrobe. He called Marlene "the most beautiful girl in the world" while keeping her happy with free marijuana and adoring words. After dating for only a week, Riley wrote Marlene a note that said:

"I am happy happy happy happy. In love love love love. Do me with me what you will."

Marlene would take Riley up on his words, seeing him as having a "kind of innocence". She did not return his love and affection at first.

"Marlene saw him as a fixer-upper," Orange said. "Maybe even as a useful idiot. She did care what people thought of her so she made him buy better clothes and encouraged him to lose weight. He would lose over sixty pounds in order to be seen as an acceptable boyfriend to Marlene."

With a new boyfriend in tow, the weirdness of Marlene escalated to another level. She identified herself as a "High Priestess of the Satanic Church". Bored during the day and out of school, Marlene would sit on her front lawn, dressed like a witch while "casting spells" on passersby.

Riley was just happy to be along for the ride. Jim Olive liked Riley at first, thinking that the shy and likable guy could be a positive influence on Marlene.

"Jim failed to see the dynamics of Marlene's relationship with Riley," Orange said. "She had all of the power. He thought perhaps that the shy, young fat kid would have some kind of stabilizing influence on Marlene. He could not be more wrong."

"There was no question that Marlene had a lot of influence over him (Riley)," Hallinan recalled. "She could make him do things."

THE LAPDOG

Riley could not believe his good fortune in scoring a young woman with Marlene's looks. Marlene, realizing the power she had in the relationship, began to order Riley to do stuff for her. She had him score free pot and steal things from stores.

Then the thought emerged that she could employ Riley to do something far bigger. She was thinking too small.

She could get him to kill her mother.

"Riley thought that Marlene was playing at first," Orange said. "It isn't like he said 'yeah, sure, I'll go ahead and do that for you. But Marlene kept badgering him and he realized that she was serious."

KILLING MOTHER

"I can't do that," Riley said.

"If you really love me you would do it," Marlene said.

"I can't."

"You can't?" Marlene asked. "You can't save me?"

"Marlene would play up her victimhood with Riley," Orange said. "She activated whatever chivalry buttons the young man had in him. He began to soften on the idea when Marlene began regaling him with the stories of abuse."

Marlene also began to soften up Riley with sex. She made him dress in all black and encouraged him to call her several times a day. When they had sex, they would have "rape" games where he would rip off her clothes. They would then further descend into kink, as Marlene would masturbate with beer bottles, a gun and even the blade of a hunting knife.

"My mother has to go," Marlene said.

"If it has to be done," Riley said. "I would die for you."

The idea of killing Naomi remained just that until Marlene's criminal activities began to escalate. She would steal her mother's credit card and max it out. The couple was then caught shoplifting on a stealing spree that netted them over $6,000 in merchandise. They were caught after being stopped for a traffic violation. The police would find the stolen merchandise as well as drugs and a sawed-off shotgun in Riley's car.

The officers then confiscated Marlene's purse and found a five-inch kitchen knife. She explained the weapon away as something she used "to sharpen colored pencils. I'm an artist."

"There really wasn't much the police could do," Orange said. "Marlene was still a minor and she represented yet another stray youth being sucked in by the drug culture of the 1970s. The police saw her as another delinquent. They would give her a hard time and try to scare her a bit.

Still a juvenile, Marlene was released to the care of her parents. Jim was lenient on her but became adamant on taking away Marlene from her "bad crowd."

"Jim was a little lenient but both parents threatened to send Marlene to juvenile hall," Orange said. "That, of course, would be a death knell to any teenager. They then forbade her from ever seeing Riley ever again and the court followed suit, filing a restraining order against Riley. Jim threatened Riley, telling him that if he ever came around the house again he would kill him. He remained steadfast in his belief that it was Riley that was influencing Marlene and not the other way around."

Naomi herself remained steadfast in wanting to send Marlene to juvenile hall.

In Marlene's eyes, this was her mother's fatal mistake.

It was time to kill her.

ORDERING THE KILL

"Get your gun," Marlene told Riley over the phone. "We've got to kill the bitch today."

Riley and Marlene made a date to kill her parents. But when the day came, Marlene made sure that her father was out of the house. She created a ruse to get her father out of the home, having the always agreeable Jim take her out shopping.

Riley arrived at the Olive residence with a pistol in a paper bag and a claw hammer.

"Riley fueled himself on drugs to calm his nerves," Orange said. "And give himself the guts he didn't have in real life. He didn't want to use the pistol because it would make too much noise and alarm the neighbors. So he planned to crush Naomi's skull in with the hammer."

KILLING TIME

When Riley first arrived he saw the family's green Vega car still in the driveway. Marlene waved Riley off, wanting him to wait until she left the home with her father.

Riley watched from a distance as his girlfriend left with her father.

She left the front door unlocked for him.

Sneaking into the home, Riley would find Naomi lounging on the couch in a drugged out state. Too groggy to put up a fight, she could only hold up her arms in meek resistance as Riley attacked with the claw hammer.

The nineteen-year-old man pounded away with the hammer, sending Naomi's blood splattering across the walls. The claw hammer then lodged in Naomi's forehead and Riley could not wrench the weapon free. He watched as Naomi writhed around on the couch, amazingly still alive.

Panicked, Riley ran to the kitchen and retrieved a steak knife. Determined to finish the job, he stabbed Naomi repeatedly with the knife.

The killing took longer than expected. Riley then panicked when he heard the Vega pull up and Marlene's father head through the front door.

Jim Olive saw his dead wife bleeding on the ground and realized that the assailant could still be in the house. He ran to the kitchen, got a knife, and began searching through the house.

He found Riley hiding behind the sofa.

"I'll kill you!" Jim screamed as he rushed the young man with the knife. Riley still had his pistol inside a paper bag, however, and he fired four shots at his girlfriend's father.

Jim Olive fell to the ground end died.

"Marlene didn't want her father killed," Orange said. "But she wasn't exactly distraught when Riley revealed that he had killed him."

Marlene looked at her two dead parents on the ground and instead focused on a portrait of herself that stood in her parent's bedroom. It was now streaked with her mother's blood.

"Curse that bitch!" Marlene screamed. "Getting her blood all over my picture!"

The two teenaged lovers did not know what to do with the body. Riley sat on the couch frozen, shocked at his own display of violence. Marlene remained calm as she came up with a plan.

First, they would go to visit friends and eat dinner out. Then they went to a drive-in movie before returning home.

They began scrubbing down the house, trying to get rid of all the blood. Marlene and Riley then rolled up the dead bodies in a rug.

"Now what are we going to do?" Riley asked. "Where are we going to put them?"

"We're going to dump them at the China Camp," Marlene said without feeling.

The China Camp was a state park near Marlene's home, an isolated stretch where they could dump the bodies without being seen.

"They soaked the bodies in gasoline," Orange said. "And burned the bodies in an open fire pit. All the while, Marlene was a cool customer, betraying no emotion as the bodies of her adoptive parents burned. She then went and had sex with Riley after they burned the bodies, giving him a reward of sorts for doing her bidding."

The two stood over the fire and watched the bodies burn.

"They should have never been married," Marlene said. "And now they're not."

The next day a hunter had seen the smoke and called in his findings, thinking that a small brush fire was starting.

Firefighters came on the scene but believed that the bones were parts of an animal. They initially believed that someone had killed a deer and burned the body.

Marlene then had a girlfriend come over and told her about killing her parents. The girlfriend then had a threesome with Marlene and Riley. A couple of days later, Marlene had a delayed reaction to the murder of her father, feeling a semblance of guilt as she cursed Riley for killing him. The guilt trip didn't last long as they then took a tour of some nude bars in San Francisco. Sufficiently turned on, Marlene performed oral sex on Riley then masturbated on top of the gear shift of his car.

"We had to do it," Riley explained to a group of friends who visited the house later. "They wouldn't let me see her."

The two then stole the credit cards off the dead bodies and treated themselves to a shopping spree and fine dining. They also went to a Yes concert.

"Here's the plan," Marlene said. "I figured it out. We're going to wait for the authorities to declare my parents dead. I'll get the life insurance. Then we'll move to Ecuador and live in luxury."

"For all of Marlene's intelligence," Orange said. "She didn't always think things through and let her evil impulses guide her. Riley did as he was told, blindly following the lead of his young paramour."

DISCOVERING THE BODIES

The next week, a business partner of Jim Olive decided to pay a visit to the house of his colleague. He wondered why the usually reliable Olive didn't show up for work or even call in.

Peeking inside the window of the home, he saw what he described as "an ungodly mess." Thinking the house had been robbed, he immediately called the police who came to the house to investigate. The police left an urgent note on the door as Marlene was not home. Confident that she could talk her way out of anything, Marlene came to the station house for questioning.

"Marlene came up with a story that didn't make a lot of sense," Hallinan said.

She told the investigators that her parents were on vacation in Lake Tahoe. What Marlene didn't know was that there was a snowstorm in Tahoe. The police informed her of that then she changed her story, going off on a tangent of having a dream about her father "in a pool of blood."

She told additional stories, none of which made any sense.

"She stated that she had no idea what happened," Police Sergeant Bart Stinson said. "But she said she knew in her mind they were dead."

The detective then had Marlene admitted to Marin General Hospital to be placed on a psychiatric hold.

He then returned to the home, finding it odd that each room had been scrubbed down. The detective did find red specks on the carpet which he determined to be coagulated blood.

Marlene was then discharged from the hospital and declared sane. The assigned detective once again interrogated her and Marlene would change her story multiple times.

First, she said that her father had killed her mother then ran away. Then she said her mother had killed her father and ran off. Another story described a burglar killing both parents and another involved Hell's Angels. Then she said her friend Diane Preger helped.

Diane Preger was then questioned by police. She said that Marlene called her over to help clean up her house. Diane recalled that there was blood all over the place.

When they finished, Diane recalled how Marlene and Riley had sex in her mother's bed.

"Marlene just has a way of making you do things," Diane said.

The police decided to talk to Marlene again. This go around, she finally came clean.

She would take the police to the pit in China Camp where they had burned the bodies.

"She tried to justify what happened based on the way she was treated," Hallinan said. "Her relationship with her mother."

Marlene informed the police that her older boyfriend, Chuck Riley, had committed the murders on his own accord. The police arrested Riley and searched his home, taking away incriminating evidence such as three gasoline cans and letters from Marlene.

"I have no guilt feeling at all about my folks," Marlene wrote in one of the letters. "NONE. NEITHER SHOULD YOU. Relax."

"She had manipulated Riley into doing her dirty work," Orange said. "But she was just as guilty as he was in pulling the trigger. When it was time to throw him under the bus, she did so without remorse."

Both were charged with two counts of first-degree murder. Marlene would describe Riley as a "madman" who murdered her parents on his own accord then he held her prisoner for a week as he sexually tortured her.

The double murder shocked the community in Marin County. The press labeled the crime as the "Barbecue Murders" in reference to the two teens burning the Olives in a barbecue pit.

Chuck Riley would be tried as an adult. He was sentenced to the gas chamber but the punishment was later commuted down to a life sentence in 1977.

The courts would be more lenient on Marlene.

"She originally was a juvenile," Hallinan said. "Had she been an adult she would still be in prison."

"It is hard to gauge how premeditated Marlene was in planning out how she would escape," Orange said. "She was clearly in a daze when talking to the cops so the drug use certainly had an effect on the wild and outlandish stories she was given. But one of the most disturbing aspects of the case is how light a sentence Marlene received. It was almost as if she knew she wasn't going to be punished severely so she had no remorse or fear."

Marlene was given a four-year sentence and was sent to the California Youth Authority for confinement and rehabilitation. But just weeks before her release, she escaped.

Marlene somehow made her way all the way to New York.

"Amazingly, she fulfilled the prediction of her mother as she became a prostitute," Orange said. "It was almost as if she were punishing herself for her crime and proving her mother correct. Or another way to look at her behavior is to realize that she thought she was punishing her mother by becoming such an evil person. She would engage in anti-social behavior when her mother was alive to piss her off and now that she was dead she would continue to do so."

"I know she got into some trouble," Hallinan said. "She went to Southern California, she got into some trouble there, there were allegations of prostitution. She got jailed and I kinda lost track of her at that point."

A REUNION

Marlene did visit Riley on one occasion in 1980.

"It was an awkward get-together," Orange said. "Chuck did the majority of the talking. He talked about how badly they screwed up and how perhaps they could help each other in the future. Marlene agreed but totally misunderstood Chuck's premise. Chuck wanted to help improve Marlene's life. She thought he needed drugs, just like old times. They were at different levels so Chuck knew that he would never hear from her again. He knew that he had served his purpose.

He literally gave up his life for that girl who now walks the streets."

"I was shy, clumsy, and inexperienced with women prior to Marlene," Riley said during a parole hearing. "I was a virgin. I fell for her completely lock, stock, and barrel into her world. I carried out these acts out of desperation driven by my selfish needs, specifically my need to be with and please Marlene in this regard of the terrible consequences for my action toward Mr. and Mrs. Olive, their families, or the community. Further exacerbating the horridness of our crime, we desecrated their bodies by cremating their remains as part of our ever growing efforts to cover up our terrible crimes. My thinking was confused and distorted. I was in complete denial that I deluded myself into acting as if this murder never happened, all a terrible nightmare to wake up from in the morning. To my core I am truly sorry and deeply ashamed for what I did, decisions I made the murder of the Olive's. I completely and utterly condemn that conduct for which there is no excuse or justification. I take responsibility for these crimes and have taken responsibility for addressing these flaws in my character to change myself to mature."

Marlene would be arrested in New York and returned to the California Youth authority where she was released at age 21. In 1986, however, she was arrested in Los Angeles for running a sizable counterfeiting and forgery ring in the San Fernando Valley. She would be convicted and sent to prison for five years.

Upon her release, she would be convicted again in Los Angeles for making a false finance statement. In 1995, she would be jailed for possessing a forged driver's license.

On February of 2003,Olive would be arrested in Bakersfield on suspicion of passing a fake check, possession of stolen property and counterfeit checks in addition to drug possession.

"Marlene Olive was incorrigible," Orange said. "She lost her good looks but she never lost her ability to manipulate people. She remained a career criminal throughout her life."

ALYSSA BUSTAMANTE

MAGGIE RAWLS

Alyssa Bustamante came from a troubled family. It sparked a rage inside of her that led to one of the most shocking killings in recent memory.

Born to Michelle and Ceaser Bustamante on January 28th, 1994, her parents were cousins by marriage and her mother was only fifteen years old. They moved around the state of California before moving all the way to St. Martins, Missouri when Alyssa was two years old. Michelle wanted to be near her mother, Karen Brooke, who lived in nearby Jefferson City.

Michelle would give birth to a set of twin boys four years after Alyssa and then have another daughter. The teen mother couldn't adequately provide for her young children, however, compiling a record of petty thefts to support a drug habit. Michelle struggled to pay the rent and found herself with three misdemeanor criminal convictions for drunk driving and marijuana possession. Ceaser was even worse, routinely beating Michelle before receiving a ten-year prison sentence for an undisclosed assault charge.

"She (Alyssa) had a very troubled background," Jefferson City reporter Jeff Haldiman said. "A very troubled life. Her mother and father both had issues with drugs and drinking."

At the age of six years old, a hungry Alyssa would walk into her living room and see her mother stretched out on the couch.

Drunk and high.

"Alyssa's mother was not much to write home about," forensic psychologist Paula Orange said. "She would do drugs in from of Alyssa, one time to the point of overdosing in front of her. She would also leave the little girl to fend for herself a lot. She was the type that would say 'there's cereal and milk in the fridge.'"

The sight of her mother down and out on drugs, the absent father, and the daily neglect would prove to be too traumatic for Alyssa.

"Something in her snapped, early on her childhood," Orange said. "There are numerous stories where children are able to overcome horrendous parenting. Alyssa received a lot of help but couldn't do it."

Child protective services would eventually intervene on Alyssa's behalf. They would remove her from her mother's custody and sent to live with her grandmother.

Her grandmother, Karen Brooke, was excited to give Alyssa a second chance at life.

"The grandmother was put in charge taking care of Alyssa and her brothers and her sister by court order due to issues that Alyssa's mother had over the years," Cole County Sheriff Greg White said.

It took some time but Karen would eventually be given legal guardianship over Alyssa and her other siblings in 2002. The children would enjoy living at their grandparents' house which was on a large ranch. There was plenty of room for the children to play both on the ranch lot and in the woods nearby.

The intervention on Alyssa's behalf, however, had come too late.

LIKE MOTHER, LIKE DAUGHTER

As she got older, Alyssa would replicate the life of her mother.

She would pop pills...Tylenol, Thorazine, whatever else she could get her hands on...then lose herself in violent fantasies and suicidal thoughts.

By the age of thirteen, those suicidal ideations would come full bore as she overdosed on some psych meds mixed with some over the counter drugs.

"It was a Labor Day weekend," Haldiman said. "When she had taken an overdose and was found in the bathroom. I think that was one of the bigger warning signs for the grandmother to try and get more help for her."

"She took a bunch of Tylenol and something else," Alyssa's friend, Jennifer Meyer said. "Some sort of pain killer. This was at her grandparent's home. She passed out and her grandma found her and called an ambulance. She had to have her stomach pumped. Then she went to the hospital for awhile and they sent her to a psych ward for awhile. I know she was away from school for like two or three months."

The suicide attempt was an alarming wake-up call for Karen Brook. Alyssa was only thirteen. Teenagers trying to commit suicide certainly wasn't uncommon among teens with troubled backgrounds, but even physicians commented that they never encountered someone as young as Alyssa with her kind of thoughts.

Karen would seek help from as many third parties as she could. She would send Alyssa to several different therapists as well as a psychiatrist who started her on anti-depressants.

A DOUBLE LIFE

Despite her inner turmoil, Alyssa was a stellar student. She never took a day off from school and got nothing less than "B" grades in school. Her teachers recognized her intelligence and she did not appear to have any discipline problems.

"If you had a face to face conversation with her," White said. "You would say to yourself that this is a good choice for a babysitter. She came across very well."

Alyssa, however, had a double life.

She would play the part of the nice high school girl during the day with conservative fashion and make-up. This fooled the teachers and counselors.

But outside of school, this would change.

Alyssa could contort her face into a hard look. She had pale blue eyes which she accented with heavy black eyeliner, drawn into a Kabuki-style triangle, giving her a clownish look. She had light brown hair which sometimes ran down into her eyes. She had plenty of attitude and ran with a Goth crowd.

She fostered this alter-ego on-line, cyber-bullying people for recreation. On her social media sites, she would smear red lipstick which she made to look like vampire blood. She would snarl at the camera and grit her teeth.

SELF-MUTILATION

The angry and bizarre poses on her social media masked a bigger problem. Alyssa hated herself and wanted to cause self-harm. She would take razor blades and make incisions on her arm and wrist.

Psychologists would see this act as a form of self-medication.

Alyssa would carve pentagrams, hearts with a line going through them, and an upside down "Peace" sign. Her largest work was carving the word "HATE" across her belly in large letters.

She would do this cutting as a form of distraction. She would focus on the blade cutting into her skin, the blood coming out...and the pain. She did this as a way to take the focus off her emotional difficulties and make physical pain take center stage.

"The cutting would give her a temporary respite," Orange said. "Alyssa would find herself coming off the high of cutting herself and eventually the bad memories, bad situations, would arise once again in her mind, forcing her to cut herself again. It would become an endless cycle of self-harm."

By the time she was a teenager, Alyssa would amass over three-hundred self-inflicted cuts all over her body. She would also burn herself with matches and bite into her skin.

"There was another side to her," White said. "It was like flipping a switch, going back and forth between the two."

"It was almost like she was living two different lives," Haldiman said. "But inside something was building up. Really building up."

AN ON-LINE PRESENCE OF RED FLAGS

Alyssa would showcase her person on-line as 'badalyssa' among other pseudonyms. In one social media profile, she listed her hobbies as "cutting" and "killing people". These were more than words of bravo from an attention seeking teenager.

Alyssa meant every word.

Her YouTube account was registered under the name Okamikage which was Japanese for "Wolfshadow." She listed her location as "somewhere I don't want to be" and her profile photo showed her with the vampire-style lipstick, pointing a finger at her head like a gun.

Scars from her cutting could be seen on her wrist.

Her YouTube channel (since removed) featured several videos of both her and her brothers trying to replicate stunts they had seen in the show "Jackass". The one revealing video, however, is one that Alyssa titled "Idiots Getting Electrocuted by Electric Fence."

The video starts with Alyssa filming herself touching an electrified fence used to house cattle. She laughs and shudders at the jolt then begins coercing her younger brothers to follow her lead.

"This is where it gets good," Alyssa wrote on the YouTube video clip. "This is where my brothers get hurt."

Her Twitter messages were all dark and more than hinted at an inner rage. She wrote often of "addiction" and "terrors."

"All I want in life is a reason for all his pain," she tweeted as well as "I hate authority."

While in school, she would freak out her friends by asking bizarre questions.

"You ever wonder what it would be like to kill someone?"

But most of her friends would not take her seriously. It seemed as it seemed like idle teenage banter.

"I was at her party," Alyssa's friend Jennifer Meyer said. "And she kind of just took me off to the side randomly and she's like, 'You know, I wonder what it would be like to kill somebody,' because I guess she was mad at one of her friends there, but it just seemed kind of strange. But you wouldn't logically think one of your friends would kill somebody."

Alyssa seemed to be building herself up psychologically to kill someone, The questions and conversations with friends allowing her to psyche herself up for something she wanted to do.

"I'd like to kill her," Alyssa would say, pointing at a random person walking down the hallway at school.

Her words would eventually lead to the deed.

THE MOST INNOCENT

Just leaving a few houses down, nine-year-old Elizabeth Olten would come over to Alyssa's house to play with Alyssa's half-sister.

Elizabeth was a sweet-faced girl with a personality to match. She loved cats, the color pink and was a "girly girl." She had long brown hair and sparkling brown eyes. She was shy but friendly.

"She was somebody special," Peggy Florence said, a friend of the family. "They call her a girlie girl. She would be outside in the snow or in the mud in her frilly little dress."

"Everything that I could tell about Elizabeth," White said. "Was that she was a sweet young lady who did relatively well at school. Her classmates seemed to like her. The teachers had good reports and her mom and family loved her dearly."

"She had frequently gone to the five-year old's (Alyssa's sister) residence," White said. "So it wasn't a huge issue."

Everyone loved Elizabeth.

Everyone except Alyssa as she watched the two girl play act with dolls on the back porch, having a "tea party."

Alyssa eyeballed the young Elizabeth with one thing on her mind. She wanted to kill her.

"I think Alyssa chose Elizabeth predominantly because it was a relatively easy target of opportunity," White said. "And that's a horrid thing."

THE KILLING TIME

In the fall of 2009, Alyssa began planning out how and when she would fulfill her sick fantasy.

She walked into the woods behind her house and began digging.

Plugging in her ear buds while listening to some death metal, she dug and dug, digging two shallow graves.

"She'd been thinking of killing for some time," White said. "And certainly had started to take significant steps toward accomplishing that end."

Alyssa dug the graves out three feet deep. Police would later speculate that she initially wanted to kill her two younger brothers and that the two shallow graves were for them. They pointed to the YouTube video in which she displayed sadistic delight in torturing her brothers by the electric fence. But when an opportunity presented itself in the form of Elizabeth Olten, she took advantage.

"Alyssa didn't care about anyone," Orange said. "Anyone or anything. She was depressed and anti-social. She hated society. She hated people."

Alyssa's diary would confirm her hatred of people and anti-social mindset. On the days leading to the murder, she would write about her cell phone battery dying. There was one long entry where Alyssa would complain about that fact that she could not call anyone to talk about the depression and rage she felt.

"If I don't talk about it," Alyssa wrote. "I bottle it up and when I explode, someone's going to die."

During this time, Karen Brooke would become increasingly worried about Alyssa. A religious woman, Karen realized that all of the counseling, therapy and medication was having no effect on Alyssa. Her granddaughter was still cutting herself and her physician raised her dose of Prozac to forty milligrams a day.

Karen would complain that the high dosage would have an altering effect on Alyssa's behavior. She would come home late when she normally would come straight home after school. She would not come down for the family evening meals, leaving her grandmother to worry about her mental state. Karen would then call Alyssa's doctor and he informed her that the higher dosage of the Prozac would take another month "to level out."

But the Prozac would have no effect on Alyssa. On October 21st, 2009, she would bring her morbid fantasies to life.

AFRAID OF THE DARK

It was starting to get dark. Elizabeth knew she had to get home or else her mother would get mad.

She said her goodbyes to her playmate then started to walk home.

Then she received a call on her cell phone.

It was Alyssa.

"Come back to the house," Alyssa said. "I have a surprise for you."

The girl trekked back to the home and Alyssa led her down the wooded path behind her home. The two walked for quite a ways before Elizabeth started to become tired and scared.

"It's getting dark," Elizabeth complained. "I want to go home."

"Don't you want your surprise?" Alyssa asked.

Elizabeth trusted Alyssa. She was older and seemed nice.

"I don't know."

"Come on, you're going to love it."

"Okay."

Alyssa put her arm around Elizabeth and led her further into the woods. The two walked and walked until the sky grew dark.

Without warning, Alyssa began to attack Elizabeth.

"Alyssa began by trying to cut Elizabeth's throat," White said. "And Elizabeth reached up and grabbed the knife, receiving defensive wounds on the inside of her fingers. Alyssa ends up dropping the knife and begins trying to strangle Elizabeth. According to her statement to us, strangling her until 'the light went out in her eyes.' And then she's down, kneeling across Elizabeth's torso and takes the knife and stabs her eight times. One time sufficiently hard to go through the breastbone, through the top part of the heart into her spine."

"This was her kill fantasy," Orange said. "That is why she tried all three methods of killing. First, she tried slicing Elizabeth's throat. Perhaps that didn't give her the feeling she craved so she began strangling the girl to death. But she needed more. She needed to know what all those fantasies felt like. So then she began stabbing the young girl. Slicing, strangling, and stabbing. She had thought about all three and wanted to know what they all felt like."

The self-harm, the self-mutilation that she practiced on herself was now transferred to harming someone else.

Someone innocent.

Her adrenaline racing, Alyssa dragged Elizabeth's body to one of the shallow graves.

"Alyssa took Elizabeth's body and rolled it to the grave and covered it up," White said. "Stringed some leaves across it and went home. Got cleaned up. Put the knife in the dishwasher."

A HAPPY KILLER

The next morning, Alyssa would write out her thoughts in her journal, expressing the euphoria at what she had done. She described how she had just killed someone, strangled them and slit their throat.

"It was ahmazing," Alyssa would write, going on to say how much she enjoyed it then ending the entry with a snarky "Kay, I gotta go to church now, lol."

Elizabeth's mother had called the police around seven p.m., about forty-five minutes after she was last seen. The community organized quickly.

The search began quickly for the girl. St. Martins, Missouri epitomized small town America. It had just over one thousand people and everyone knew each other. Volunteers began searching the woods behind the neighborhood homes.

Police pinged Elizabeth's cell phone and the GSP led them to the woods but the battery on Elizabeth's cell gave out.

The authorities knew they were close but they could not find Elizabeth.

Alyssa had done a very good job of hiding the body.

"Elizabeth was already dead before we were ever notified," White said. "It was that fast."

Everyone in town thought that an older male predator had snatched up Elizabeth.

"That was the narrative that everyone was used to," Orange said. "Everyone became frantic, talking about any strangers that they may have seen in town. But soon rumors spread that a teenager was involved. Everyone assumed it to be a teenage male."

RETRACING ELIZABETH'S STEPS

Alyssa had not shown up for school the day after Elizabeth's abduction. It was her first unexcused absence.

This raised a red flag to police as they questioned Alyssa. They brought her out back where they asked why she had dug out a grave.

Then they began searching through the house.

Alyssa acted fast. She tried to block what she had written in the diary by scratching out the words.

"We were still able to read some of the words through the writing," White said. "We put a very strong light source behind it and read her original words. At that point, she did confess to it and ultimately take us to the scene of the homicide and to the grave."

Word spread around town that Elizabeth was dead and that Alyssa was the killer.

Everyone involved went into shock. A senseless crime, a murder of an innocent.

Did this really happen?

The brutality of the crime shocked the community. An adult killing a child is rare but it has happened before. No one had ever heard of a fifteen-year-old girl killing a nine-year-old.

"When they announced they had found the body," Haldiman said. "There was an audible hush. They just couldn't believe that, nobody could believe that, number one a child was dead and number two that the person that did it was as young as she was. That just floored so many people. Everybody."

The case became even more tragic as only weeks earlier a panel of psychiatrists determined that Alyssa should be institutionalized for a long term. These clinicians knew that Alyssa was an extreme danger to both herself and other people.

Their warnings went unheeded, however, and Alyssa was returned home.

THE TRIAL

Alyssa would be put to trial and be tried as an adult.

"In this case," White said. "It was clearly, coldly planned, calculated and executed. She executed her neighbor for no reason other than she wanted to see someone die."

While awaiting trial, Alyssa went stir crazy behind bars. She began cutting herself with her own fingernails before placed on suicide watch. Her attorney motioned that she be sent to a psychiatric institution.

Her defense team worked overtime to try and explain Alyssa's murderous act. They recounted the fact that she had been on the anti-depressant Prozac and had been told to increase her dosage a few weeks before murdering the little girl. They told the jury about her upbringing of neglect, suicide attempts and the mental illnesses/drug use of both parents.

But the community-at-large wanted Alyssa's blood. Among the things they wrote were:

"What is a shame is that the Murderer did not die when she tried to commit suicide when she tried to in 2007."

"From what I've heard this girl has had mental problems for some time and has seen counselors or someone in the past."

"Either deport her or send her to the gas chamber. One less sicko wasting our tax dollars."

Prosecutor Mark Richardson would argue for Alyssa to receive life in prison plus an additional seventy-one years.

The years that Elizabeth had lost.

"These sentences are appropriate," Richardson wrote. "And fit what happened to Elizabeth at the hands of a truly evil individual who strangled and stabbed an innocent child simply for the thrill of it."

Alyssa would plead guilty to second-degree murder.

She would take the stand during her trial and betray some signs of humanity, turning to Elizabeth's mother and family.

She expressed how "horribly" she felt for what she had done. Then she suggested that if she could give her own life for Elizabeth's, she would.

The apology fell on deaf ears for both Elizabeth's family and the jury. They felt as if the apology was fake and meaningless.

"I think Alyssa should get out of jail the same day Elizabeth gets out of the grave!", screamed Elizabeth Olten's grandmother.

"She's an evil monster," Elizabeth's mother, Patty Preiss said. "So much has been lost at the hands of this evil monster. Elizabeth was given a death sentence, and we were given a life sentence. I hate her. I hate everything about her. She's not even human."

"Alyssa was pure evil," Orange said. "She told investigators that she killed Elizabeth, that darling little girl, because she wanted to see the light in her eyes go out. If that doesn't make her evil and irredeemable, I don't know what does."

"When a person plans and executes for no other reason that they want to see another person die," White said. "That person is going to re-offend. I think Alyssa is too dangerous to be out of prison.

Alyssa would be sentenced to life in prison but given the possibility of parole. She currently resides in a Missouri women's prison.

Elizabeth would receive the funeral of a beloved princess. Her casket was placed inside a horse-drawn carriage.

All of her friends and family wore her favorite color: pink.

WHEN THE GIRL NEXT DOOR KILLS: THE TRUE STORY OF TYLAR WITT

ERICA FOSTER

"At round one in the morning, the girl snuck the boy into her house. He stabbed her in her sleep, killing her and freeing themselves." This was an excerpt from fourteen year old Tylar Witt's story entitled, "The Killer and his Raven." A story she wrote about her own mother's brutal murder.

Tylar Witt lived in an upscale neighborhood in El Dorado Hills, California with her forty seven year old single mother, Joanne Witt. Joanne worked for the county as an assistant engineer for the Department of Transportation and they lived in an elegant house in a nice gated community. Tylar was a fourteen year old girl who was entering her freshman year at Oak Ridge High School. She was described as a sweet girl when she was growing up. Her mother paid for riding lessons and they liked to stay at home and watch movies and cook, but as Tylar grew up, the behavioral problems began and the fights between the mother and daughter turned into physical altercations. Tylar was turning into a different person, she was becoming a monster.

It all started out as what looked like typical teenage rebellion. Tylar embraced the emo and gothic lifestyle by wearing dark and baggy clothes, she had a love of anime and Japanese cartoons, along with everything violent and connected with death. Tylar met her 'Romeo', nineteen year old Steven Colver, at a coffee shop in the popular shopping center of Town Center Shops, where they both frequented. As Tylar was entering her first year of high school, Steven was beginning his first year of college. He was employed as a Shift Lead at Rubio's Mexican Grill. The duo quickly became inseparable. Tylar looked at the older boy as a god and worshiped everything about him. There wasn't anything she wouldn't do for him. The two were in love.

It was in April of 2009, a few weeks after the two had met, that Tylar approached her mother. She convinced her mother that Steven was gay, so that he would be allowed to rent the extra room in their family home. After much resistance from family and friends, Joanne defended the decision by saying that Steven would be helping her make the mortgage payment, as well as help Tylar with her homework. She was described as very strong-willed by her friends and family and didn't let their opinion of others affect her decision to let Steven move in. Joanne didn't suspect a relationship between Steven and her daughter until one day in May, about a month after Steven had moved in. She entered Steven's room and found Steven and Tylar about to engage in a sexual relationship, or had just finished. She found Tylar naked and hiding in Steven's closet, trying to cover herself up. Joanne was understandably upset and demanded that Steven immediately move out. She called two of her male coworkers to come over and assist her. Joanne informed them that she was kicking Steven out of her house and she didn't want to be alone when she did it in case anything were to happen. The male coworkers helped place all of Steven's belongings on the sidewalk and even threatened Steven before he left.

Vinnie Capatano, one of Joanne's coworkers helping her that day, threatened Steven, "If you make contact with Tylar again, either by phone or in person- I am going to hurt you. And I am going to hurt you East Coast style, not West Coast style." It was an act intended to promote intimidation and scare tactics. Steven looked unshaken, which annoyed Capatano even further. His words didn't seem to bother Steven at all.

Joanne was convinced that Steven had committed a crime by sleeping with her underage daughter and made that clear to Steven before he left. She threatened to go to the police and file statutory rape charges if Steven ever came into contact with her daughter again. He didn't take Joanne's words seriously, or the threats of her coworkers. Steven was later found at least twenty more times after this encounter, sneaking into Joanne's house. All Joanne wanted to do was get her daughter away from this older boy that seemed to influence her bad behavior and irrational decisions. Joanne acted as any other mother in this situation would.

Despite the threats, Steven and Tylar continued their love affair and sexual relationship during the day while Joanne was at work and late at night while Joanne was sleeping. Joanne had expressed concern to a few of her coworkers about her daughter's behavior and the boy that seemed able to control and influence her so greatly. It wasn't long until Joanne found out what was going on behind her back and continued to make good on her promise of going to the police. Steven and Tylar vowed to find a way to stay together, no matter the cost. This is the moment the plotting began between the modern day Romeo and Juliet. This was about a month before Joanne Witt was found dead in her home and arrest warrants were issued for her daughter and her daughter's boyfriend.

Joanne Witt located her daughter's diary and handed it over to the police that were handling the statutory rape complaint. The diary clearly outlined the sexual relationship between Tylar Witt and Steven Colver. It explicitly described numerous sexual positions and encounters that the two had shared. There was no mistaking that there was definitely a sexual relationship happening between Steven and Tylar. The detective called to interview Steven about the allegations and Steven claimed that he was worried about Tylar, but their relationship was platonic. He said he considered Tylar as more of a sister figure, than anything else, and he denied any sexual relationship between the two of them. He also admitted that he was scared of this whole situation and he knew she was only fourteen years old. The relationship between Tylar and her mother was volatile and destructive, to say the least, even before she turned in the diary.

Joanne was a loving and attentive single mother that made her daughter, Tylar, the center of her world. However, an incident that took place when Tylar was five years old, prompted an investigation that removed her only daughter from her home. Tylar was placed into foster care for a brief time before Joanne's parents, Norb and Judi Witt could take her in. Tylar lived with them for 6 months while Joanne attended anger management and parenting classes. The incident occurred when Tylar was just five years old after

Joanne had picked her up from daycare. The young girl was screaming in the backseat which was causing Joanne to lose patience very quickly. Joanne reached back and slapped Tylar. The daycare saw the hand shaped mark on Tylar and immediately reported the abuse to CPS, Child Protective Services.

After Tylar was finally able to go back home to her mother, Joanne was afraid to discipline her like she had before. This gave Tylar the opportunity to do whatever she wanted, knowing she could get away with it. Tylar would threaten to call CPS and report her mother again if she didn't get what she wanted. This created many behavioral problems for Tylar and this manifested itself in the violent relationship between the mother and the daughter. Tylar also reported that her mother was a heavy drinker and she would hit and punch Tylar when she was mad. These allegations were never proven. If the violence and abuse had been as severe as Tylar had made it sound, there would have been noticeable marks and bruises on Tylar. They never found any evidence of the abuse she claimed was taking place at the home. There was constant fighting and arguing. Joanne didn't feel comfortable enough start disciplining her daughter again until the few months before that led up to her murder.

The day that Joanne admitted to taking her daughter's diary into the police, was the same night that Joanne and Tylar got into a horrendous fight at home. Tylar felt betrayed by her mother's actions and began throwing objects at her and fighting with her. Tylar called 911 pretending to be Joanne in an attempt to be taken out of the home. She would have rather been in the Juvenile Detention Center than at home with her mother that night. Joanne got onto the phone with dispatch and when they asked her if she was okay, she responded no. Deputies were on their way to the residence. When the police arrived they saw a cut on Joanne's chin and several bruises. Tylar was taken in that night but was released only hours later, after Joanne refused to press charges against her daughter. Joanne was never required to go to the hospital due to her injuries.

Norbert Witt, Tylar's grandfather, claimed that Steven was a bad influence on his granddaughter, and said that he corrupted her by exposing her to sex and heavy narcotics. Steven was known to engage in illegal narcotics such as marijuana, ecstasy, and cocaine.

Norb and Judi Witt owned a luxury RV and had spent the previous two months traveling around the country. They arrived home only days before they received the call that would turn their world upside down. It was Monday when they received a call from Joanne's boss inquiring if they had any idea as to the whereabouts of their daughter. Joanne had an impeccable work history and never missed work without first calling to let them know. So, when Joanne didn't show up or call that Friday, her coworkers began to worry. They stopped by her home that night and knocked on the door, but there was no answer. Nobody seemed to be home. After Joanne didn't show up to work the following Monday either, they knew something was terribly wrong and called the police to report Joanne as missing. After speaking to Joanne's parents and informing them that they had already contacted the police, they raced over to their daughter's house, which was only a few miles away, so they could check themselves. It is there that they met the police. Norb Witt let them into the house to search. The police informed Joanne's parents that she was found upstairs in her room, and she was deceased. There was no sign of a break in or forced entry, there was nothing missing in the home. But where was Tylar? Better yet, where were Tylar and her older boyfriend?

It didn't take the police long to realize that Tylar and Steven had something to do with the cruel and heinous crime in the Witt house. It was only weeks earlier that Joanne had reported Steven to the police and turned in Tylar's diary. She made her feelings about her mother known in the words scrawled throughout the pages. Tylar even plastered her contempt for her mother across her social media sites. She wasn't shy when it came to sharing her feelings and opinion of her mother.

Tylar and Steven went on like normal the days following the murder. They were living the life they wanted now that Tylar's mother wasn't there to get in the middle of it and stop it. They were seen holding hands and kissing, and had seen some of their friends. It was after a night of smoking marijuana and doing lines of cocaine at Steven's father's house that Steven confessed to murdering Joanne and even showed his friend the bloody knife that he was hiding in the car. This friend was Matthew Wildman. Wildman later testified against Steven and told the court that Steven did indeed show him the knife that was used, and he described how the murder happened, and how Steven stood there when he was finished and watched Joanne die. Steven's father came home unexpectedly so they all left the house, with the murder weapon. The murder weapon was never retrieved after their arrest.

The couple had fled to San Francisco, they no longer cared about the consequences because their plan all along was to commit suicide. If they weren't there, they wouldn't have to face the murder charges. According to their logic, that was the only way that they would be able to stay together, without interference, as well as keep Steven out of jail because of the statutory rape charges. They thought the charges would carry a heavy prison sentence and they didn't want to risk separation due to the diary that Joanne had turned into the police earlier.

While in San Francisco, they rented a hotel room and consumed a bazaar mix of fruit loops, cake and rat poison and each had written out suicide notes. The combination of food mixed with the rat poison didn't work, however, and they were arrested shortly after, before they had a second chance to commit suicide. Alongside the food that was found in the hotel room, police also found marijuana, condoms, Steven's work apron and nametag, and the movie 'Donnie Darko' on DVD. They were found changing clothes behind a dumpster at a shopping mall in the area and were arrested by local police and taken in for questioning regarding Joanne Witt's murder.

Once in custody, Tylar refused to admit that she knew her mother was dead and admitted no fault. She asked for a lawyer and for the detectives to go away. The fateful night her mother was brutally murdered was June 11, 2009. Well into the night, after Joanne had finally fallen asleep, Tylar let Steven into the house. He had acquired a chef's knife from his restaurant job at Rubio's. Tylar had grabbed a knife out of the kitchen in her house, and the two proceeded to go upstairs to the bedroom where Joanne Witt was fast asleep. They had each planned to use the knives they had to kill Joanne....together. Tylar claimed that she could not go into the room with Steven. She fell to her knees and covered her ears, while humming to drown out the sound of her mother being stabbed to death. Steven had taken several practice slashes in the air as a warm up before going into Joanne's room and Tylar said this is what prompted her to stay outside of the room. She chose not to go in with Steven. Joanne was stabbed around twenty times. The fatal wound was a gaping slash in her neck. She struggled with her killer and had put her hands up in defense but the wounds were too severe. A bloody knife outline was left on the bed and a book entitled, "How to Parent your Out-Of-Control Teenager, was ironically nestled in the nightstand next to her bed. Tylar and Steven covered Joanne's body with a blanket, turned the air conditioner down in an attempt to preserve the body, and locked up the house and left. They decided to jump the fence instead of having to put the code in to get out. They didn't want anyone to place them there at the time of the murder.

In a suicide letter that Steven had written to his friends, as a kind of apology for what he had done, he said, "Our souls are tainted...We shall be awaiting our fate in the afterworld."

After the news of Joanne's murder got around, a neighbor spoke up about allegedly speaking to Tylar in the park a few months prior. The neighbor had been walking her daughter to the park and claimed she saw a young girl that looked alone, sad, and even angry. The girl was sitting on the swing set with her face toward the ground. She confronted her and asked what was wrong. She said the girl described a bad home life with her mother, and mentioned that her mother liked to drink and would get violent and hurt her, and they would get into a lot of fights. She said the girl seemed really cold and lost in her replies. When asked what Tylar was going to do to stop it the next time it happened she simply replied, "There isn't going to be a next time. Next time it is going to be either her or me." This statement stuck with the neighbor for a long time after. When she realized that the crime scene was a daughter that killed her mother, she finally spoke to police about the conversation in the park. The neighbor was seen on news footage talking to one of the police on the scene, but requested that her name be left out of the media.

Dan Weiner, Steven's attorney, claimed that it was not Steven that committed the murder, it was Tylar. When describing her relationship with Steven, Tylar said, "I trusted him more than I trusted anyone. And I love him more than anybody or anything. If he told me to jump off a bridge and I asked him why and he said just trust me, I would have done it." This shows just how much influence Steven had over Tylar. When neighbors of Steven's were asked to describe him they had only nice things to say.

"He's always been a nice kid as far as I am concerned. If this is true, it is out of character." –Paul Matloff. He also described Steven as a stand-up kid that never played his music too loudly and was always eager to help his neighbors.

Joan Colver, Steven's mother was quoted by reporters as saying, "He would care about others before himself. Steven is the kind of guy who would drive off a cliff or jump in front of a bullet or run into a burning building....for a friend."

When asked why Weiner felt that Steven was being targeted for performing the actual murder instead of Tylar, he didn't really know why. He backed up his defense and Steven's statement of Tylar being the one to murder Joanne Witt, given her past history compared to Steven's.

"He has never hurt anybody, or tried to hurt anybody or threatened to hurt anybody. As contrasted with Tylar who has a very specific history with her mother, and has literally threatened to kill her, to stab her...the very method by which she was ultimately killed!"

Steven had changed his story and said that Joanne was already dead by the time he arrived at the Witt house that night.

"I think realizing the gravity of the situation after being in jail for a while, it took a while before he was willing to confirm, yeah, that she had done it and how she had done it."

Steven said that Tylar stabbed her own mother to death and then called him over to the house after it was done. That is when he claims to have seen the bloody knife. He said that there was blood dripping everywhere, including some spots on Tylar's pants, but there was no evidence of blood droplets being found anywhere else in the house. It was all confined to Joanne's bedroom where she was murdered. The defense claimed that the police failed to look for blood anywhere else except for the primary focus of the house, which was the bedroom. Therefore, there was no evidence available to back up Steven's story. This new story also came about after Steven had already described to his friends how he stabbed his girlfriend's mother to death in her sleep with a butcher knife. Weiner said that Steven was not homicidal, rather suicidal. They claimed that the plan was for Steven to pick up Tylar and they would run off to San Francisco for a few days and then commit suicide together. There was no talk of murdering Joanne. The defense also mentioned that Steven had a clean record, while Tylar's was filled with a history of violence and running away. Despite the new story, Steven's confession to his friend was more than the prosecution needed. He was convicted based on his own words, just as his mother had predicted earlier.

In prosecutor Lisette Suder's words in her opening statement at trial, she described the couple's actions as "a

19 year old man and a 14 year old girl and their love affair that led to the violent almost to the point of sadistic murder of her mother." Tylar was portrayed as an extremely manipulative and brilliant girl. After lying to the detectives when she was first taken into custody and questioned, she finally decided to tell the truth and later passed a polygraph test proving it. She admitted to conspiring with Steven to kill her mother, but also said that it was Steven that committed the actual murder, while she lay in a fetal position outside of the bedroom. All of the evidence found on the scene corroborated Tylar's account of the events from that night. Tylar, in exchange for her testimony against Steven, received a reduced sentence of fifteen years to life for second degree murder. She would be eligible for parole at the age of twenty nine, instead of thirty nine. They were both sentenced at the El Dorado County Superior Court in Placerville.

Joanne Witt's brother, Michael, shared his feelings before sentencing. He was the one that had been responsible for cleaning up his sister's home after the murder. He said he would never be able to get the images of the crime scene photos out of his head.

"I hope and desire that Mr. Colver experiences the worst possible experiences our wonderful prison system can bestow upon him." The judge had tried several times to stop Matthew's rant.

The trial began with Steven still trying to protect Tylar. He didn't want people to accuse his love, Tylar, of being the mother killer. In the beginning stages of his questioning he would ask investigators if they had spoken with Tylar and he inquired about her well-being. He was sympathetic to her situation and just wanted to help her. He thought they were in it together and their love would keep them connected. It ended with the scorned lovers passing the blame to each other. Steven's defense referred to him as an easily manipulated love-struck teen.

Steven's trial lasted for four weeks but the verdict only took four hours to come back. With Tylar's account of the events, the confession Steven made to his friends, and the DNA found underneath Joanne's fingernails that linked the homicide to a male attacker, it all led Steven to a verdict of guilty, for first degree murder. He was sentenced to life in prison without the possibility of parole.

After sentencing, however, Tylar had an interview in which she admitted, "I still have a really hard time being honest. I panic when I get in trouble and the first thing I want to do is lie to get out of it." This statement could potentially be enough to seek an appeal for Steven Colver at a later date. It showed just how dishonest Tylar could be. So if she were able to say this now, what if everything she said in the trial was a lie, despite the polygraph test.

Tylar's psychologist referred to her as a sociopath. Tylar, in trial, said she had three different personalities that were living inside of her. She had her own personality, an angel named Alex, and a demon she referred to as Toby. She claimed her violent actions that led up to this point were because of the demon. Toby would come in times of intense stress. Tylar also described blackouts that she would experience when she was enraged and tried to use the compassion of her dead mother to sway the jury in her favor.

"My mom was not a vicious person and she didn't hold grudges. Even if something horrible like this would have happened, she would have asked for a just punishment. She wouldn't want to see someone suffer for the rest of their lives for a mistake they made when they were being ignorant and stupid."

The following is a letter that Tylar allegedly wrote to her mother before she was murdered. It was Tylar's plan to run away and commit suicide. It was a good bye letter addressed to Joanne.

"*As much as you don't think I love you, I do. Not just because I am your daughter but because you are my best friend. Nothing I have ever said to you in anger was ever true. I would never kill you or hate you....but I can't stand to see you so unhappy, but I am growing up and seeing as you don't love me....the person I have become, I see it only fit I do one last thing to make you happy. You want me gone? I am gone.*"

In Tylar's testimony she admitted the act of violence toward her mother was not a spontaneous decision. It was a decision Steven and Tylar had made after thoroughly discussing their options.

"I was in shock and then I went into a full blown panic attack, hyperventilating, screaming, and shaking." This was in response to Tylar finding out that her mother had turned her diary over to the police in an attempt to build a case against Steven. They came to their own realization that the only way to save Steven from jail was to murder her mother. There was no way they wouldn't file the charges after all the proof was in the diary. They didn't see another way out.

Steven and Tylar concocted this murder plan, afraid that Steven would be sent to prison for a long time because of the statutory rape charges Joanne had filed against him. They didn't want to risk being separated from each other. They saw the murder and subsequent double suicide as a way of staying together. Just like Romeo and Juliet. What they didn't know was that the statutory rape charges only carried a year worth of prison time, if there was any time at all; it was considered a misdemeanor. Instead of a small charge, with little or no prison time, they exchanged a lifetime of freedom for a lifetime of being locked away due to their irrational nature and horrid actions that were compelled by fear. Neither Tylar, nor Steven were able to determine exactly which one of them came up with the idea of killing Joanne. Tylar had been labeled a liar from the very beginning but all of the evidence they had matched with what Tylar had been saying about that night. Everything fit into place and that's why they believed she was finally telling the truth about Steven.

During Tylar's sentencing the judge addressed her directly, "This was a brutal murder. The court has seen no emotion or even remorse for the loss of your mother...I'm sorry for you Miss Witt, because the person who loved you most and without reservation is gone."

Judi Witt had waited a long time before she would go and visit her granddaughter. When she finally set eyes on Tylar she asked how she could have done such a horrible thing. A look of shock plastered across Tylar's face and she responded, "Do you really think I would have been able to do something like this?" When asked if Judi actually believed her, she responded yes.

Not only did they lose their daughter, Judi and Norb Witt also lost their granddaughter. Judi was able to forgive a little easier than Norb. Norb has since written his granddaughter off for killing his daughter. Her actions were inexcusable. She is not the same little girl that they remembered. They said that the Tylar they knew, wasn't the Tylar that killed Joanne. They choose to remember the little girl that they first visited in the hospital after her birth. Tylar was their third grandchild. They recalled the hospital visit after her birth very fondly. They walked in there with a camera and took many pictures, in awe of their own daughter and their new granddaughter. They choose to remember Tylar as the little girl they had watched grow up, not the monster she had become after killing her own mother, not the girl that constantly defied her own mother and threatened her. Not the girl that wrote in her diary about her dream of finding out her mother had died in a car accident. Tylar had lost her way a long time ago. They choose to only remember the good, but revealed that their family was never going to be the same either. Judi and Norb had come to terms with this.

Norb finally decided to go and see Tylar, after the trial. He had refused to go and see her up until this point. When Norb entered the room, Tylar called him Poppa and embraced him. She began sobbing. Norb held onto her tightly and said, after speaking with her, he could see some kind of remorse for what she had done but he still wasn't in the position of being able to forgive her. "It is hard to forgive someone that helped kill your daughter." Norb and Judi do not visit Tylar in prison, but they do say they write to her very often.

In later interviews Tylar finally began showing small signs of remorse for her mother's brutal ending. At one time Tylar had even considered her mom to be her hero and looked at her as not only a mother figure, but also as a father figure, since she never had a real father. Tylar's personalities were all over the place. She would love her mother one day but threaten to kill her the next.

Steven's mother still holds onto the hope of her son's innocence and the possibility of an appeal. She refuses to believe that the boy she knew would be capable of doing something so unforgivable and so violent to someone else.

The tragic death of Joanne Witt and the story of her daughter and her daughter's boyfriend being the murderers shook the community. A violent history with Joanne and her defiance of any kind of authority figures led Tylar into the arms of someone she felt could protect her. The two scorned lovers had a premeditated and thought out plan to kill the object of their resistance. According to their teenage logic, getting rid of Joanne and committing suicide was the only way they could ever be together. Even the most thought out plans tend to backfire, however, and they were very much alive while Joanne was gone. They traded a life of freedom with some restrictions, for a life spent behind bars. They miscalculated the situation and now live to regret it, day after day, year after year.

WHEN GIRLS NEXT DOOR KILL : THE TRUE STORY OF MELINDA LOVELESS

IRIS OWEN

"Melinda Loveless is the closest thing you will ever look at and know what the devil is. Her eyes are empty. There's nothing inside of her." - Jacqueline Vaught, mother of Shanda Sharer.

BIRTH OF A MONSTER

Melinda Loveless was born on October 28th, 1975 in New Albany, Indiana to Marjorie and Larry Loveless. Melinda would be the youngest of three daughters born to the couple. Her father, Larry, would be a celebrated Vietnam veteran who would be given a hero's welcome in his return home. Behind closed doors, however, Larry was a certified nut who abused his wife and children.

After returning home from military service, Larry would work for the Southern Railroad before becoming a probationary officer with the New Albany Police Department. He would be fired after only eight months on the job after he and his partner would be convicted of assaulting an African-American man.

Larry would justify the assault as he believed that the man slept with his wife.

The incident would be a bit of a head-scratcher as Larry had fantasies of being a cuckold. He would bring his co-workers home to have sex with his wife so he could watch. He would also introduce his wife to a swingers lifestyle.

Larry was a hedonist. He indulged in whatever pleasurable whim his mind could dream up. This also meant spending exorbitant amounts of money. He would buy motorcycles, cars, guns, and other gadgetry. It all became too much as the couple would file for bankruptcy in 1980.

Seeking to turn his family's destiny around, Larry decided they needed religion. He would gather up Melinda and her sisters to attend the Graceland Baptist Church. Both Larry and Margie vowed to stop drinking and put an end to their swinging lifestyles. Larry would soon become a recurring speaker in the church, taking the podium and talking about how Christ had changed his life.

Bad judgment would remain at the forefront of their lives, however. They would let Melinda go with an older man to a hotel room by herself as he claimed he needed to perform an exorcism on her. Larry would become one of the resident family counselors in the church. He would talk to a troubled husband and wife privately and invariably make a pass at the women. He tried to rape one of them and was then excommunicated from the church.

After that incident, Larry decided to turn his back on religion and anything that resembled taking the high road in life. He and his wife would then resume their partying ways with booze and swinging.

CRIMINAL PERVERSIONS

Larry would state that he and his wife had an open relationship. They would enter bars together in Louisville and Larry would pretend to be in the medical field, acting like a big shot doctor or dentist. He would introduce Marjorie as his girlfriend but proceeded to hit on whichever bar girl caught his eye. He would also allow some of his friends from work to have sex with Marjorie but she found his co-workers to be repulsive.

They would have sex orgies with other couples. On one occasion, Margie tried to commit suicide afterward as the experience was so degrading.

Undaunted, Larry would direct a gang rape of Margie and she again tried to kill herself by drowning. She would deny Larry sex for over a month until one night he became so frustrated that he raped her in front of Melinda and her sisters.

Yet she remained with him.

Around 1986, the couple were again in a seedy Louisville bar with Larry chatting up two women. He wanted to take the women home but Margie would not let him. Enraged, Larry would beat his wife up so bad that she was sent to the hospital. He would later be convicted of battery.

By 1988, Larry began working for the United States Postal Service but quit after three months. He loafed around on the job and would often bring undelivered mail back to his home to burn. With little money coming in, visiting extended family would often complain that the Loveless daughters looked undernourished.

INCEST

The rumors about Larry sexually abusing his daughters remain uncorroborated. There were court testimonies that he had fondled Melinda's older sister Michelle when he was a baby. There were also allegations that he molested his wife's thirteen-year-old sister as well as Melinda's cousin for several years.

Melinda's cousin would testify in court that Larry tied all three sisters up in the garage and raped them on by one. Both of Melinda's sisters have said that he molested them but Melinda herself would not admit that it ever happened to her.

She would, however, sleep in bed with him until she was fourteen when he finally left the family.

What is certain was that Larry had a traumatizing effect on all of his daughters. On one occasion, he fired a gun in Michelle's direction when she was only seven, missing intentionally but trying to scare her. He would also take the girls' underwear from the laundry and smell it in front of family members, trying to humiliate them.

Margie would then catch Larry "spying" on a then fifteen-year-old Melinda and her friend. Enraged, she grabbed a knife and began slicing at him. He was able to wrest the knife away from her but had to go to the emergency room for injuries suffered during her attack.

"Margie had an inability to cope," forensic psychologist Paula Orange said. "She tried religion, counseling, hedonism. It all didn't work. Larry was a pervert with a personality disorder. He would run right over Margie and do whatever the hell he wanted. This traumatized Melinda obviously. Her father was abusing her and others while her mother's only response was to try and kill herself."

Margie would try and kill herself one last time but her daughters were able to intervene. Larry would then divorce Margie, wanting to start a new life. He left behind all of his daughters, remarried and moved to Florida.

Melinda took her father's absence the hardest. Larry would humor her for a little while, writing her letters.

Soon the letters stopped and their relationship deteriorated to having no contact.

"The divorce would have a great impact on Melinda," Orange said. "Her home life was horrid, obviously. She had no guidance other than her mother's Christian fundamentalism which would be offset by the way she lived her life. Melinda was raised by spiritual schizophrenics if you will. What she ultimately did was her choice but she did not have any sort of checks and balances in place when she was a child."

Melinda's father, Larry, would be arrested in February of 1993 after open court testimony revealed that he had abused his wife, daughters and their cousin. Because most of the crimes took place between the years of 1968 to 1977, all but one of Larry's charges would be dropped to the statute of limitations in Indiana. He would plead guilty to one count of sexual battery then be released in June of 1995.

He then tried suing the Floyd County Jail system for $39 million dollars. Among his primary complaints during in incarceration was that he was now allowed to sleep during the day or read the newspaper.

His lawsuit was unsuccessful.

THE DOWNWARD SPIRAL

Melinda's behavior became increasingly erratic after her father's rejection. She would get into fights at school and exhibit signs of clinical depression. At the age of fourteen, she entered into a lesbian relationship with a classmate named Amanda Heavrin. Her mother expressed anger at Melinda's sexual orientation but would eventually accept it. Melinda's relationship with Amanda, however, would eventually deteriorate.

The two were not dating when Amanda would become enamored with a younger girl named Shanda Sharer. Melinda would see the two talking outside a school dance and go into a jealous rage.

What she didn't know was that the fifteen-year-old Amanda was smitten with the twelve-year-old Shanda.

Amanda, both looked and dressed like a young boy. She cultivated a "boy band" look and had a sweet disposition that put Shanda's guard down. Shanda was a lonely wallflower at the school. She had recently transferred in and did not have any friends yet. Amanda took advantage of the situation, sending the young girl love notes, flowers and calling her one the phone.

Shanda liked boys but Amanda remained persistent. She knew that Shanda was flattered by the attention and grateful for her company. The new school was a lonely place for the young twelve-year-old.

Their friendship turned into a romance.

And Melinda Loveless could not have that. Amanda was hers and hers alone.

SHANDA SHARER

Shanda and Amanda would spend an increased amount of time together as the school session wore on. When they weren't together, they were writing each other notes or talking on the phone. Shanda's mother, however, caught wind of the relationship and did not approve. She thought Amanda was too old to hang out with Shanda, who was only twelve. The fact that Amanda was a lesbian only raised her eyebrows further.

Shanda was born in Pineville, Kentucky on June 6th, 1979 to Stephen Sharer and Jacqueline Vaught. Her parents would divorce early in her childhood and Shanda would move with her mother to Louisville when she remarried. Shanda would excel in school, receiving good grades while participating in cheerleading, volleyball, and softball. Her mother would divorce again when she was twelve and the family would move to New Albany, Indiana. She would then transfer into a Catholic school after her parents worried about her relationship with Amanda Heavrin. While at Our Lady of Perpetual Help, Shanda played on the basketball team and proceeded to get her life back in order.

"I met her in junior high," Amanda Heavrin recalled. "We became very, very close. We became really good friends."

But Amanda's feelings toward Shanda would only enrage Melinda. Shanda was the passive recipient of Amanda's attention but Melinda didn't see it that way. She would send Shanda notes, one of which read:

Amanda and I are going together and she loves me and I love her and she only wants to be friends with you. You need to accept that! You need to find you a boyfriend because Amanda is mine.

"Shanda would go up to the teacher's desk and Amanda would be staring at her," Melinda said. "I'd see her and Amanda laughing and passing notes and I'd get mad."

The jealousy would eventually come to a head at the school dance. Melinda saw Shanda talking with Amanda outside and immediately confronted her young rival.

"She tried to beat Shanda up," Amanda said. "I got between them and told Shanda to run."

Melinda would be distraught afterward. She began a letter writing campaign to Amanda.

"I want Shanda dead," Melinda wrote.

"I didn't think she was capable of murder," Amanda said. "I thought maybe she'd just try to scare her. Beat her up or something. That's the Melinda I knew. I didn't know her as being a violent person."

TEEN GIRL KILL SQUAD

Melinda wanted Shanda dead.

With murder on her mind, Melinda would enlist the aid of three of her friends. Laurie Tackett, Hope Rippey and Toni Lawrence. Three teenage girls who all had similar, troubled backgrounds. The amount of psychiatric medications prescribed to each of the four teens would be enough to supply a psych ward for a year...and together they would make for an uncontrollable, unpredictable mob.

Together, they would drive over to Shanda's house and listen as Melinda told them of her plan.

But who were these girls that were so easily persuaded to murder?

First, there was Laurie Tackett, born in Madison, Indiana in 1974. She came from a religious family as her mother was a fundamentalist Pentecostal Christian. Taking on extremist views, her mother attempted to strangle Laurie when she found out that she was changing into jeans at school. Her mother also came to Hope Rippey's house unannounced after finding out that Hope's father had given the girl's a Ouija board. She then demanded that the board be set on fire and that Hope's house should be exorcised.

Laurie's father was a convicted felon who worked in a factory. She would later claim she was molested at the ages of five and twelve. Child protective services became involved and would come to Laurie's house unannounced to ensure that she was not being abused.

Laurie would rebel against her parents and would take a profound interest in the occult. She would entertain her friends as she would pretend she was "Deanna the Vampire", acting as if she were possessed.

She would enter into a lesbian relationship at the age of seventeen and her girlfriend would introduce her to self-harm. Her mother would discover her self-mutilating scars and check her into a mental hospital. Laurie would be prescribed anti-depressants upon her release but would slice her wrists again only days later. She would then be diagnosed with borderline personality disorder after a second stint in the psychiatric ward.

Having no goals or concern about the future, Laurie would drop out of high school

An elementary school friend of Laurie, Hope was born in Madison in 1976. Her parents would divorce when she was eight and she would move with her mother and siblings to Quincy, Michigan. Her parents would get back together, however, and the family would return to Madison in 1987. She had grown up with both Laurie and Toni Lawrence and was happy to be reunited with them. Her parents were leery of Laurie, however, and wanted Hope to steer clear from her. Like Laurie, however, Hope was troubled and begin to self-harm at the age of fourteen.

Toni Lawrence rounded out Melinda's trio of killers. She was born in Madison in February of 1976. She would be molested by a relative at age nine and later raped by a teenage boy at age fourteen. The boy would not be charged with the crime, instead, the police only issued a restraining order. Toni would go into therapy after the assault but refused further treatment after a couple of sessions. She would later begin to self-harm as well as sleep around with other boys, getting a reputation as a "whore". She would try to commit suicide in eighth grade.

The stage was set as Melinda had assembled a group of young girls that were just as damaged as she was. Girls that were ticking time bombs. Alone they would have done nothing violent. But together? Together they would be capable of the most horrific crime imaginable.

"Everything that horrible that happened to each of those girls," Shanda Sharer's mother, Jacqueline Vaught said. "Everything that happened to them, they took it out on my child. I think that's what they were doing, I think they just all exploded that night."

The four teenagers drove around the Indiana back roads as Melinda detailed her plan. Laurie was in the driver seat as she was the only one old enough to drive. All piled in, Melinda would tell her acolytes of her plan to scare a girl named Shanda. She pulled out a kitchen knife from her jacket and showed it to the girls.

She's a copycat," Melinda said. "I want to scare her for stealing my girlfriend."

"I'm tired of hearing you just talk about hurting her," Laurie said. "If you really want to hurt her you should go ahead and really do it."

Melinda took the challenge. She needed a volunteer to lure Shanda out of the home. She knew that Shanda's parents were no longer allowing her to see Amanda anymore. But if they could use Amanda as bait, they could lure her out.

Melinda knew Shanda's address but the girls got lost a few times and stopped to ask for directions.

Finally arriving at the home, Melinda sent Hope Rippey to the door.

Jacqueline Vaught came to the door and saw Hope in front of her. She had never seen the teen before but didn't think anything wrong when Hope politely asked if Shanda was home.

"Shanda had never been anywhere where we didn't know where she was or who she was with," Vaught said. "Shanda was not allowed to go to anybody's house where I didn't call the parents that I didn't go there. I was very, very protective."

She called Shanda down and left the teen girls alone.

"Your friend Amanda is upset and really needs to talk with you," Hope said.

"Why?" Shanda whispered, looking back to make sure her mother wasn't listening. She was no longer allowed to have anything to do with Amanda.

"She's waiting for you at the Witches Castle."

Shanda knew that Hope was referring to an old, stone house, located on an isolated hill next to the Ohio River. It was a creepy but teens like to hang out there.

"I'm having nothing more to do with Amanda."

"Have a heart," Hope said. "You must care about her, couldn't you be there for her just one last time?"

"Why did Amanda send you instead of coming herself?"

"Amanda knew she couldn't come to your house."

"I can't go now," Shanda said, looking behind herself again. "My parents are up. I'll sneak out around midnight if you want to come back hen."

Hope agreed and returned the car without Shanda.

Melinda immediately confronted Hope on why she didn't have Shanda with her. Hope explained that Shanda agreed that if they came back at midnight, she'd be willing to come with them.

The teens then head out to a nearby punk rock concert. Both Toni and Hope get bored and have sex with two boys they've just met to pass the time.

Midnight rolled back around and the girls returned to Shanda's home.

"I can't wait to kill Shanda," Melinda said. "I'd like to fuck her."

Melinda then hid in the back seat. The other girls covered with a jacket and trash from inside the car.

Hope then went and got Shanda.

"They were not mean looking, dirty child molesters," Shanda's mother, Jacqueline Vaught said. They were two children that looked like her. They said just walk twenty-five feet and talk to her. And that's what she did."

Shanda squeezed into the front seat, sitting in between Laurie and Toni. The girls pretended to like Shanda at first but soon she began feeling uncomfortable.

"The Witches Castle is a short drive away," Laurie said. "You know the legend? That house had once been owned by nine witches who had controlled the town and the townspeople had burnt the house to get rid of the witches."

"So what's up with you and Amanda?" Hope asked, turning to Shanda.

"We'd been going out for quite awhile," Shanda said. "I really cared about her."

"I see."

"What's wrong with Amanda?" Shanda asked. "Why does she have to see me so badly?"

"Surprise!" Melinda screamed, jumping out from the backseat. She grabbed Shanda's hair, pulled her head back and put the knife to the young girl's throat.

"Please don't hurt me," Shanda said.

The girls all laughed.

Laurie stepped on the gas...

CRUEL AND SADISTIC

"Bitch," Melinda hissed as she pressed the knife down on Shanda's throat. "Don't move, don't make a sound."

They arrived at the Witches Castle, parked and pulled Shanda inside. Melinda tied up Shanda's hands with a rope. Hope waved the knife in front of Shanda's face, taunting her. Laurie took along an old t-shirt and set it on fire.

"You see that?" Laurie held up the burning shirt before the crying Shanda. "That's what you're going to look like before the night is over!"

Melinda then ripped off Shanda's necklace and bracelets. She handed them to Toni and they took turns admiring the items. Hope ripped off the Mickey Mouse Musical watch from Shanda's wrist and put it in her pocket.

Several cars passed before the castle and then the girls went quiet, waiting for the coast to clear. Not satisfied that they would have total privacy, the girls dragged Shanda back to the car and stuffed her in the back seat, covering her with a blanket.

Laurie made a pit stop at a gas station while Melinda stood guard over Shanda. Hope went inside to pay for the gas while Toni makes a phone call.

She does not tell the person she is calling about the kidnapping or ask for help.

The girls then go back to their hometown of Madison, Indiana, an hour away.

Once there, they drove a few miles past Laurie's home and pull off into a seldom used logging road. Laurie stops the car and they all get out. Hope and Toni complain about the cold and wait inside the vehicle.

Melinda then hauled out Shanda from the back seat. The girl resisted until Laurie came to help and they muscle her out of the vehicle, throwing her to the ground.

"Take your clothes off, bitch," Melinda screamed.

Crying, Shanda complied with the request. Hope and Toni watch from the car window.

Melinda then took Shanda's clothes and threw them into the back seat. "I want them as souvenirs.

Playing along, Hope put on Shanda's polka dot bra. Toni turned on the radio.

"Shanda had hugged me," Laurie said in a December 1992 interview. "She asked me not to let Melinda do it. She was crying. There wasn't anything I could do."

Laura instead held Shanda's hands behind her back. Melinda then began punching the little girl.

"Please let me go," Shanda screamed. "I'll stay away from Amanda."

"Shut up!" Melinda punched Shanda hard in the stomach. She followed this up by pulling her by the hair as she fell to the ground. Shanda was prone and Michelle repeatedly kneed her in the mouth

Shanda winced and yelped in pain.

Her adrenaline and nerve increasing, Melinda took out her knife and tried to cut Shanda's throat. The blade is too dull, however.

"Get over here, Hope!" Melinda commanded.

Hope obeyed and Melinda ordered her to help hold Shanda down. Melinda then tried to use her foot to pierce the knife through Shanda's throat.

The girls then took turns stabbing Shanda in the chest.

The knife was still too dull.

"We need to just strangle her," Laura said, taking the rope and wrapping around her neck.

"Please don't kill me," Shanda pleaded.

Melinda just laughed. She sat on her Shanda's legs as Laura straddled her chest, tightening the rope.

Shanda would pass out and the girls thought she died. They picked up her body and tossed her in the trunk of the car.

POINT OF NO RETURN

The girls would arrive at Laura's home, triumphant. They would go upstairs to Laura's bedroom and drink soda. Laura, the occult aficionado, would take out her "runes stones" and perform a "future reading" for the girls.

"Our futures look good," Laurie said until they heard her dog barking outside. The teens rushed to the window and listened. They could hear Shanda screaming from the trunk of the car.

Laura went to the kitchen and got a paring knife. She hurried outside, opened the trunk and began stabbing Shanda repeatedly. The girl quieted down and Laurie closed the trunk again.

Laurie returned to her bedroom, covered in blood. She washed herself up and then addressed the kill squad with a renewed need for cruelty.

"We have to go for a ride," Laurie said.

"I'm tired," Toni said.

"Me too," Hope agreed.

Melinda and Laurie dismissed the girls and went for a drive by themselves. They headed back to the isolated road, parked and then went to check of Shanda had died yet.

The little girl sat up. Her eyes rolled in the back of her head. She tried to speak but was only to say one word.

"Mommy."

AN ENDLESS NIGHT OF TORTURE

Laurie picked up a tire iron from the trunk and bashed Shanda across the head. She closed the trunk again and they drove along the back roads. The mood turned somber and silent until they once again head Shanda choking in the back trunk.

Laura stopped and got again, opening the trunk and bashing Shanda in the head the tire iron once more. This time, a chunk of flesh from Shanda's temple went flying into the night air.

Laurie came back to the car, blood splattered across her arms.

"She looked as though she was painted red," Laurie laughed, waving the bloody tire iron and under Melinda's nose who smelled it with glee.

Melinda and Laurie then go back to Laurie's home. The woke up Toni and Hope, laughing and filling them in on how much further they tortured Shanda. The foursome discussed what they should do with the body until Laurie's mother woke up.

She berated her daughter for being out so late then yelled at her even more for having her friends spend the night without asking.

After her mother's lecture ended, Laurie led the girls to the back of her house.

ONE LAST ACT OF EVIL

"There's a burn pile out here ," Laura said, skipping through the woods beyond her back yard. They would find the burn pile but it would be covered in frost.

"That won't work," Laura said. "We're going to need some gasoline."

The girls went back to the car and opened the trunk, needing another look at their victim.

Toni refused to look at the tortured body of Shanda, shocked by the amount of blood covering the girl.

"Start the car and rev the engine if she starts screaming," Laurie said.

Hope grabbed a bottle of Windex in the trunk and began spraying Shanda's body.

"You're not looking so hot are you?" Hope taunted.

Shanda was semi-conscious. She sat up, her naked body covered in dried blood.

"Laurie!" Laurie's mother called out.

"Shit," Laurie slammed the trunk lid on Shanda's head and went to find out what her mother wanted.

After a few minutes, Laurie returned and the girls drove to a gas station. Laurie ordered Toni to buy a two liter Pepsi bottle from inside. She came back and Laurie emptied the bottle into the dirt then filled it with gasoline.

"We could get rid of her out by Lemon Road," Hope offered.

Laurie followed Hope's directions, driving onto the old country logging road. Toni would remain in the car as the three other girls pulled Shanda out from the vehicle.

Hope would pour the Pepsi bottle filled with gas over Shanda. Laura lit a match and tossed it on the body.

The fire blew high. The girls giggled and ran back to the car, speeding away.

"Wait," Melinda said. "Turn the car back around."

"The way it was told to me," retired detective Steve Henry said. "Was that they drove away and turned around and came back past the body thinking that she would be burned completely up and there would be no trace of her and she was still there so Melinda set her on fire again."

Laurie complied, doubling back and stopping in front of the burning body. They watched for a few minutes until Melinda stepped out of the vehicle with the Pepsi bottle.

She looked down on Shanda, her body in a fetal position. Tongue lolling in and out of her mouth as she convulsed in pain.

Melinda poured the remainder of the gas on Shanda and tossed another match on the little girl.

The teens then drove off and ate breakfast at a McDonald's.

"What does this remind you of?" Laurie asked as she held up a piece of sausage.

"Shanda's body," Melinda laughed. "Burned to a crisp."

Shanda was not dead yet, however. Soot was later found in her airways which meant that she was burning in the fumes around her. She was conscious while they set her on fire.

"They didn't know how to tell me how she died," Shonda's mother, Jacqueline Vaught said. "And I saw it on television. That she'd been burned alive. I didn't know that."

Melinda would then call her ex-girlfriend, Amanda Heavrin and confess to the crime.

"She told me everything that happened," Amanda recalled. "I thought it was a joke. Because I just cannot fathom that four little girls would do this to another human being. This is stuff you wouldn't even do to an animal."

She thought that if she removed the competition that she could have Amanda.

CONFESSION AND TRIAL

Toni Lawrence would be the girl to come forward and confess. She came home hysterical, telling her parents what happened. They took her down to the police station and she told detectives what happened.

All four teenagers would be charged as adults. This forced them to accept plea bargains as they wanted to avoid the death penalty.

The defense played on the fact that all four girls were victims of physical and/or sexual abuse in their childhood. Hope, Toni, and Laurie had histories of self-harming behavior. Laurie was clinically diagnosed with a borderline personality disorder and had both visual and auditory hallucinations.

Toni would cooperate in exchange for a lesser sentence. She was allowed to plead guilty to one count of criminal confinement which got her a maximum sentence of twenty years. Hope would be sentenced to sixty years with ten years suspended for mitigating circumstances plus ten years of medium-supervision probation. She would continue to appeal and the judge would reduce the sentence to thirty-five years. Both Laurie and Melinda wold be sentenced to sixty years and sent to the Indiana Women's Prison in Indianapolis.

Melinda's attorney would appeal for her release in October of 2007. He would argue that Melinda had been "profoundly retarded" by the abuse she suffered during childhood. He further argued hat she had not been competently represented during her initial sentencing. He also played the "age card", as Melinda was only sixteen years old when she entered the plea agreement with the state of Indiana and needed consent from a parent or guardian.

The appeal for her release was denied but the sentencing was reduced down to make her eligible for parole in fifteen years. It is becoming apparent that Melinda and Laurie could be released from prison as early as 2022.

Toni would be released from jail in December of 2000 after serving nine years. She would remain on parole until 2002. Hope was released from the Indiana Women's Prison on April 28, 2006, serving for fourteen years.

"None of these girls were born murderers," Vaught said. "They weren't born to murder children. They weren't born to be in prison. This what we do as parents. We mold our children into what they are."

Shanda's father, Stephen, would die at the age of 53 due to alcoholism. Stephen had become depressed over the death of his daughter and subsequently "drank himself to death" over the years.

"Steve could not have been a prouder father," Vaught said. "Shanda was his life. From the day that she died he did everything he could to kill himself beside put a gun to his head. And finally he drank himself to death and he died at fifty-three."

"Melinda has cheated me out of being with my daughter during this life. It is my wish for you (Melinda) that you live your life with memories of her screams and sign of her burned and mutilated body. I hope and pray you remember these words for the rest of your life: May you rot in hell."

WHEN GIRLS NEXT DOOR KILL : THE TRUE STORY OF CINDY COLLIER & SHIRLEY WOLF

IRIS OWEN

"Today, Cindy and I ran away and killed an old lady. It was lots of fun" -
Shirley Wolf's journal, June 14th, 1983.

Shirley Wolf and Cindy Collier met in a juvenile detention center and had known each other for only a few hours when they decided to escape and randomly kill a stranger.

They would go to a senior condominium center in Auburn, California where they would seek an elderly victim.

They would find one in the eighty-five-year-old Anna Brackett. They entered her home under the ruse that they needed to use the phone to call their parents.

The girls would brutally murder the elderly woman in a crime so shocking that deputy sheriffs were initially in denial that two young girls would commit such a crime.

But how did they get to the point mentally where they could commit such a horrid act? This is the story of how they got there.

EARLY LIFE

Cindy Collier wasn't the nice girl next door. Her entire body language spoke of rage and hostility. By the age of twelve, she was a regular at the juvenile hall where she would routinely assaulting staff and inmate alike.

Incorrigible, she had been arrested for burglary, theft and drug possession.

Because of her age, Cindy was often spared jail time and was sentenced to community service. She would most often be sent to pick up litter on highways but the punishment wasn't enough to deter her from a life of crime.

"She was a smart ass towards everyone," former classmate Mike Fluty said.

No one was spared her rage. At fourteen years old, she had no problem harassing adults as well, randomly accosting people on the street.

"What are you looking at?" she asked a woman walking by as she smoked a cigarette. "You think you're better than me?"

She would then raise her fist to the woman and force her to run away. "Oooh!" Cindy taunted. "Ooooh! Come on, you want some?"

"Cindy liked to intimidate," forensic psychologist Paula Orange said. "She had learned it was better to be a predator than the prey very early on in life. Her early childhood would shape the monster she would become."

Cindy's parents divorced when she was one year old. Her mother would remarry but that would end in divorce as well. She would take care of Cindy and her three sons during the day and go to a waitress job at night.

Cindy stated that she had been raped by an undisclosed family member and by another man who threw her down a flight of stairs after he finished with her.

"Her mother reportedly had different children all by different men," Orange said. "Cindy was molested by one of her mother's endless string of men that she brought into the home."

Cindy would talk about her "rotten" childhood and describe being "raped a few times." She tried to commit suicide on several occasions but that only brought her more frustrations. So instead of harming herself, she decided she would harm others.

"I want them to pay," she said.

By the time she entered Chana High in Auburn, California, Cindy had a well-established reputation of someone who should be feared. Using physical intimidation, she would randomly choose a girl she didn't like and the bullying would begin. She would push and yell, getting in their face. Her victims would be spared no quarter, on one occasion, Cindy ripped the blouse of a girl and forced her to run down the street topless.

"She was a trained bully," Orange said. "She knew exactly how to push the buttons of her victims, strip them of their dignity. It was done to her at home so it was easy for her to pass along the abuse."

Cindy was a menacing presence on campus to the other petite girls. At 5'9" and 140 pounds, she could beat up any girl in the school. She had a strong jawline and broad shoulders but it was her eyes that set her apart from the average bully. Eyes that pierced through her victims and gave them an implicit message.

I want to kill you.

Cindy's crimes would not be limited to physical assaults. She would grab and take whatever she wanted. She would go into liquor stores, stuff food into her pockets and leave. She would go into malls and steal cassette tapes at the record store. After a few months, she graduated to stealing a car. This would land her in a juvenile detention center where she would be a kindred spirit unlike any other she had met before.

LIKE LOOKING INTO A MIRROR

Like Cindy, Shirley Wolf had been the victim of sexual abuse. Her father, Louis Wolf, would rape her. But the abuse didn't stop with just her father. She was a molested by her paternal grandfather and uncle as well.

An observant kindergarten teacher noticed the odd behavior of Shirley and recommended that she get psychiatric help to no avail.

Shirley didn't know where else to turn as she would be abused by all of the men in her life. At the age of six years old, she had run away for the first time. The streets were too rough for her, however, and she was scared back home by the dark characters of Brooklyn.

A lost little girl with nowhere else to go but the house where she was abused.

Her father, Louis, worked as a carpenter but suffered an accident that forced him to take disability. He would remain at home and begin bossing his children around. Then it turned to the sexual abuse of his daughter, Shirley.

When Shirley was around six, the family would move from the east coast to Placerville, California so Louis could be closer to his own family.

Louis Wolf would send Shirley's mother Katherine on an errand to get some groceries one morning. He then locked Shirley's three younger brothers out of the house and turned his attention to Shirley.

He cornered her in the bathroom and raped her.

Shirley would never forgive her father for what he did to her.

Louis would rape his daughter sometimes as much as three times per day. By the time she reached puberty, he put her on birth control.

Shirley never told her mother because she didn't want to break up the family.

Louis would tell Shirley to not tell her mother what he had done. Shirley obliged only because she was afraid how badly the news would hurt her mother.

Eventually, however, the abuse became so intolerable that she told her mother.

Her mother suspected it all along. She then went to the authorities.

Louis would deny that he molested Shirley but plead guilty to reduced charges which brought his sentencing down to a mere one-hundred days.

Louis was told that if he fought the charges, he would be facing fifty years. So he took the three months.

Shirley would then be removed from the home which was her worst fear. She would be bounced from foster home to foster home where she told of feeling "like a stranger."

"You get to the point where you're pushed in a corner and I just came back fighting," Shirley said. "I want to go home. I forgive my father and I try to forget it. He's apologized to me, my family and to God."

A MATCH TO A FLAME

It would be only fitting that the first time the girls would meet, it would be under the guise of violence.

At the detention center, Shirley was being beaten to a pulp by a fellow inmate in the hallway. As per usual, no guards were around. But Cindy stood her ground against the bigger girl, to no avail.

The girl threw her against the wall, punched her in the stomach and twisted her arm.

"Who are you?" Cindy asked as she came upon the two girls fighting.

"Shirley Wolf."

"I like you, Shirley Wolf."

And with that, Cindy got her opponent into a full nelson, easily overpowering Shirley's tormentor.

"Let her have it," Cindy said.

Shirley didn't hesitate. She began pummeling the girl, all of the rage of being abused all of her life came forth as she gave the girl a beat-down.

Cindy threw the girl to the ground and the two laughed as she moaned in pain.

"Later loser," Shirley sniffed.

Cindy laughed. The girl had spunk and they spent the next couple of hours exchanging their life stories.

For some reason, Cindy did not feel hatred toward Shirley. She felt like they had an unspoken bond but she didn't know why.

The truth was, they were both ticking time bombs.

"I think it was an unfortunate chemistry between the two girls," Shirley's defense attorney Thomas Condit said. "I think it also had to do with finding a new friend and wanting to show that she was capable of doing anything that the friend was."

Shirley was the opposite of Cindy in one regard, however, as she did not have Cindy's assurance. Shirley felt "hopeless and helpless" as she talked about running away from the detention center. She talked about this as if it were an impossibility, a faraway dream.

But Cindy felt otherwise. She behaved as if she knew all the answers.

"I can get us out of here," Cindy said with total assurance.

"You can?"

"Sure. I do it all the time. But we're going to need a car. This place where I used to live as all kinds of old people. We can steal one of their cars. But we'll probably have to kill them."

"Yeah," Shirley said.

"You know," Cindy said. "In case one of them rats us out."

Cindy led the way as the girls escaped. They talked about how they would put their sadistic plan in motion. They wanted to find someone old and feeble...someone who could not fight back...someone who they could kill for fun.

"I suppose a good analogy would be to compare the girls to the boys from Columbine who would come over a decade later," Orange said. "One needed the other to pull off such a horrid act. They needed that voice over their shoulder to egg them on. They both wanted the same thing and together they could make it happen."

Both Cindy and Shirley would dye their hair red in order to disguise themselves. They then went "victim hunting," touring Cindy's old neighborhood in Auburn Green, a condo for senior citizens. They wanted a car. A nice one. So they began searching the parking lot for a car and would match the number on the parking slot to the condo number.

Then they would knock on the door. Their questions were innocent. They would ask for directions, a glass of water or ask to use the phone. But there was something about their demeanor, a sinister or insincere look in their eye that set off the alarm bells for all of the senior citizens they met. They were allowed inside by Joe Becker and his wife who gave them a glass of water. When they left, however, the elderly couple immediately washed the glass and scrubbed the phone with alcohol, the girls seemed so dirty.

"They were looking for an easy target," Orange said. "Becker was seventy but still probably too much of a hassle for them. They needed easy."

Then they knocked on the door of Anna Brackett.

"We decided we were going to kill her when we saw her," Shirley said. "She was just an old lady. Just a perfect setup. We killed her because we wanted her car and we didn't want to get caught."

Anna was a retired seamstress who worked for Sears. She had great-grandchildren who were the ages of Cindy and Shirley.

She was a helpful and kind person to all her knew her. She didn't hesitate in helping some girls that were the ages of her great-grandchildren.

"Can I help you?" Anna opened the door with a smile.

"Hi," Cindy said. "Can you please help us? We need to call our parents and the phone down the street is not working."

"Sure," Anna said, opening up her door.

Ann was congenial and didn't see any reason not to trust the girls. She let them into her home and the threesome chatted for over an hour. They sat on the couch and she gave them soda. She would show the girls pictures of her family. Pictures of her children, grandchildren.

"It is unusual for a sociopath to want to know about their victim," Orange said. "They really don't want to know their victim because it humanizes them. So perhaps the teen girls were hesitant at first. But it was more of a case of them working up the nerve to do what they set out to do."

The phone rang and Anna went up to answer it.

The call came from her son.

"I'm on my way," her son said.

"Okay," Anna said, hanging up the phone. "I'm sorry, girls. My son is coming to pick me up. We're going to the bingo parlor."

"Now," Cindy said as the girls pounced.

Shirley grabbed the elderly woman by the throat and slammed her to the ground.

"What are you doing?" Anna screamed. "What are you doing?"

Cindy sprinted to the kitchen and rifled through the drawers. She found a butcher knife and gave it to Shirley.

"Do it," Cindy commanded.

Shirley would then stab the helpless old woman without mercy. She would recall stabbing her in the neck and "freaking out" because the old lady kept screaming.

"You're killing me!" Anna shouted.

"Good," Shirley said, slicing the knife down again. She would stop only when she saw the blood coming out of Anna's mouth.

Anna Brackett would suffer over twenty-eight stab wounds although the coroner believed it could have been more as the blade went through the same entry point. There was one stab wound where the blade had gone in four inches deep past Anna's breastplate.

"She died a horrific death," Orange said. "Painful and horrific. I've read some psychiatrists say that Shirley was getting revenge on all of the people that hurt her in the past, that in some way Anna symbolized her mother and she was killing her mother symbolically. I believe that is psychobabble. Shirley was not that bright. She was following the lead of Cindy and they wanted to kill and maim. That was the point. Not to subconsciously work out her anger. She was a defective unit."

Cindy then sifted through all of Anna's drawers and closets looking for money. They found the keys to the old woman's 1970 Dodge and ripped the two telephones from the wall.

They went into the garage and found out that the keys they had stolen would not start the car. Angered, they left the condo on foot and began hitch-hiking.

Ironically, Anna's son Carl would drive pass them on the street, ignoring the girls who had their thumbs out.

He then entered his mother's home and discovered her mutilated body on the floor.

It was a surreal scene for her son. His mother on the floor in a pool of blood. Trapped in his own real life horror movie, Carl would never have guessed that two underage girls would be capable of such a thing.

LIKE A DAY AT THE OFFICE

Cindy and Shirley made it to her home in Auburn. They turned on the television, eagerly awaiting news of the murder they had committed.

Too many people had spotted them around the neighborhood. In all, eleven people informed the investigating officers of the two red-headed girls with the strange demeanor.

Some remembered Cindy from when she lived with her grandparents in the condo development. The deputies, however, didn't believe that two teenage girls could have done what they did to Anna.

Back home, the girls would cheer as their murder was reported on the evening news.

Then they went to sleep.

At 2:30 a.m the deputies would arrive at the house of Cindy Collier.

Deputy George Coelho didn't believe the girls did the crime. But after a few minutes of questioning, Shirley confessed.

Cindy, however , would not only confess to the crime, she would gloat.

"She started to laugh," Deputy Coelho said.

Cindy expressed little remorse. She told the deputies that she felt like killing more people.

Shirley was excited and giddy as they had done something that "they had never done before."

They were placed under arrest and one of the deputies began reading her the Miranda rights. Shirley interrupted him, repeating the rights verbatim as she was already familiar with the process.

Cindy would tell the police that she felt jealousy toward anyone who appeared happy and normal. She felt such envy that she wanted to kill them.

The deputy expressed shock as Cindy detailed her desires of wanting to hurt people. She bragged about stabbing, shooting and throwing people into the Auburn Damn. The officers knew it was all bravado...with the exception of what they did to Ann Brackett.

The two girls would go to trial in July of 1983...a juvenile court.

What the girls wanted was fame and publicity.

They would get it as the brutal murder would be talked about in numerous high-profile magazines and the court case would reach a national audience. A movie called "Fun" was produced, chronicling the girl's first day together.

CRIME AND PUNISHMENT

Shirley's attorney, Thomas Condit, would enter a plea of not guilty by reason of insanity. "I'd like to say that Shirley felt sorry," Condit said. "But I can't. That's part of her problem. She told me that while she was killing the old lady, she was thinking of everybody she hated—her father and his mother. But the psychiatrist believes it was a symbolic killing of her own mother."

Both girls would receive the maximum imprisonment for underage girls. They would remain in jail until the age of twenty-five then be released.

"Shirley really can't understand the difference between right and wrong," Condit said. "How do you appreciate right and wrong when you have a father telling you it's wrong not to stay home and service him when you should be in school?"

THE AFTERMATH

Cindy would spend the next nine years at the California Youth Authority facility in Ventura. She would obtain an associate of arts degree then go on to study law at Pepperdine University. She would go on to have four children and live in Northern California without any further brushes with the law.

Shirley would be sent to the Central California Women's Facility near Chowchilla.

She would threaten other inmates and her jailers during her time in prison. She spent her days reading romance novels as she tries to take her mind off the tormented childhood which led her to be capable of such a crime.

"I think of my dad and it hurts," Shirley said. "I'll just feel pain and I'll have to cry to get it out. I can't really pinpoint where it's from. God knows, I'll get hurt and just cry."

Shirley would complete her high school education and become a born-again Christian. The attempts to improve her life would prove futile, however.

She had tried to contact her parents but they never returned her calls or letters. Finally, in the summer of 1992, Shirley tracked down the number of her parents in the Pacific Northwest. Louis, the man who had molested her, would answer her call.

They had not spoken in four years but he had told her that her mother had left him a few months prior, leaving the three young boys with him. Shirley asked about her favorite brother, L.J., but her father avoided giving her a straight answer.

Shirley wanted desperately to know what happened to her younger brother but could not locate him anywhere. Her father would then stop returning her calls.

On June 30th, 1995, Shirley would be freed from prison after serving twelve years for the murder of Anna Brackett.

Her father would die in 2002.

Unlike Cindy, Shirley's life of petty crimes would continue. She would get involved in prostitution, theft, and burglaries. She has shown remorse for the murder but also stated that "there is no going back."

Both women are now free, getting leniency for the crime because of their age. Their light sentences would draw the ire of Anna's son, Carl, who would rage at the judicial system that gave his mother no justice.

KILLER TEEN : THE TRUE STORY OF KRISTINA FETTERS

JANET NIXON

Kristina Fetters was the youngest woman in the state of Iowa to get sentenced to life in prison without parole after she murdered her great-aunt. But eighteen years later she would be re-sentenced after the Supreme Court ruled that mandatory life sentences for minors was unconstitutional.

Kristina would later be released to a hospice center as she developed breast cancer in prison.

But what happened that fateful night of October 25th, 1994? Kristina was only fourteen years old, five-feet tall and barely one hundred pounds. Yet she committed one of the most brutal assaults in the history of her Iowa town.

This is what transpired in her life before and after she committed a brutal murder of her loving aunt.

EARLY LIFE

She was born Kristina Joy Fetters on February 5th, 1980. The product of a biracial union between her mother Darlene and an African-American man, Kristina did not get to know her father growing up.

Instead, she spent her childhood with Arlene and Wayne Klehm. They were the great-aunt and great-uncle of Kristina but she thought of them as her grandparents. She would refer to Wayne as "Uncle Sheenie" and to her aunt Arlene as "Pooper."

Kristina would play at their home as a young child, swinging from bedsheets tied to a tree in the front yard of the couple's one story home.

Wayne was the easy going one of the couple. Arlene, on the other hand, was the one who enforced discipline on the precocious Kristina.

But Kristina was close to her aunt as were all of her other cousins. Arlene was described as a 'spitfire', a woman who spoke her mind.

"Arlene was just a tiny framed, little woman that would tell you exactly where to go and how you could get there," Kristina's cousin Shanna Sickles said.

Kristina would not meet her biological father until she turned eight years old. She wanted a close relationship with him but the bond never materialized.

"I want him in my life," Kristina said to the Iowa Register in 1996. "I need him in my life. I don't think he knows what he wants."

RUNNING WITH A BAD CROWD

Kristina seemed to have little guidance in her early life. At only twelve-years old, she would meet a twenty-three year old African-American man from Milwaukee named Anthony Leon Hoover. He was a gangster "wannabe", seeking membership into a street gang called the "Black Gangster Disciples." Immature and naïve to the perils of the street, Kristina told the man that she was seventeen years old and ran away with him.

But in June of 1993, Hoover would be arrested on kidnapping charges. He held Kristina at gunpoint, broke her nose and then raped her.

Kristina could not cope with the trauma inflicted by the older man. She would not go to school and would runaway on a weekly basis.

By January of 1994, she was so troubled that she was sent to the Orchard Place, an unlocked facility for minors with behavioral problems. Kristin was placed on Prozac and underwent treatment.

"She was on three different medications that are well known to not play well together now," her friend Jaimi Ross said. "She was showing every warning sign, every red flag that you possibly could on these drugs and they were all ignored."

She also sought solace in Christianity to no avail. A Polk County Juvenile Court officer said that Kristina "lived in a fantasy world most of the time."

Her mother, Denise, would support this assessment as she described her daughter as having hallucinatory episodes.

"She'd say 'look, look, there's Johnny. He's laying on the floor," Denise said. "There's a knife in his head. He's bleeding. Somebody help him, somebody help him. And the teachers would try and re-direct her, you know, you need to get up here and finish your homework."

In September of 1994, her Uncle Wayne would die. Aunt Arlene then sent her grand-niece a handwritten letter, trying to smooth things over.

"Let's be nice to each other and forgive me if I hurt you," Arlene Klehm stated in the letter.

But Kristina would not take the olive branch of her great-aunt.

PLOTTING A MURDER

Ten months later, on October 25th, 1994, Kristina and her roommate Jeanie Fox escaped from the Orchard Place.

Their destination was Kristina's great-aunt's home in Polk County, Iowa.

Arlene Klehm was 76-years old and had little contact with her grand-niece since her placement into the mental health facility.

Living in her fantasy world, Kristina concocted the idea that her aunt Arlene had a lot of money. She planned to escape from the facility, kill her aunt and ride off into the sunset in her truck. What her plans were beyond that, she didn't know.

All she knew was that she needed a partner in crime.

First, she approached a girl named Jessica Wilhite. She explained that her aunt had a lot of money and it would be an easy kill. They could take both her money and her truck after doing the deed.

Jessica remained non-committal.

Kristina then went to Tisha Versendaal and told her of her plan.

"She sits in a chair all day," Kristina said. "I'll stab her then cut her throat. She keeps her money in a safe. We'll take all her money then get away in her truck."

But she found no taker in Tish who was due to leave the facility soon. Instead, she settled on Jeanie Fox, who wanted out of the facility.

Telling Jeanie her plan of escaping and leaving the part of killing her aunt out of the equation, the two packed their bags. They left the facility without incident and that is when Kristina told Jeanie of her other plans.

"Do you want to come with me to kill my aunt?" Kristina asked.

A FIELD TRIP TO MURDER

The girls stopped at three different homes before heading off to kill her aunt. The final stop was at the apartment of a friend where Kristina got a small paring knife.

"What do you need that for?" the friend asked.

"I'm going to kill my aunt," Kristina laughed as she left the apartment.

The two girls arrived at Klehm's home and noticed that a van was parked outside.

Her aunt was entertaining company.

Kristina wanted to wait as she didn't want any witnesses.

The two girls then knelt behind a fence and waited for her aunt's friends to leave.

"I am going to fucking kill her," Kristina repeated the sentence like a mantra outside the home. "Satan has given me the power to do so."

Her aunt's visitors finally left and the two impatient girls knocked on the door. The old woman let them both in, unsuspecting of what the girls had in store for her.

The three small-talked in the kitchen before Kristina pulled Jeanie into a side room.

"I'm going to fucking kill her," Kristina said, again like a mantra as if she were psyching herself up.

Gathering up the nerve, Kristina marched into the kitchen where her aunt was sitting and smashed her over the head with a tea kettle.

Arlene fell to the ground. She tried to get up, woozy, and asked what happened.

Kristina showed no mercy. She exchanged the kettle for a heavy metal skillet and smashed it across her aunt's head.

"Give me the knife," Kristina called out to Jeanie.

Taking the paring knife, Kristina tried to slice Arlene's throat but the knife wasn't sharp enough. She then rummaged through the kitchen drawers, found a larger knife and stabbed her aunt in the back.

"Anthony!" Kristina cried out with every stab (according to Jeanie). "Anthony! Anthony!"

"Help!" Arlene wailed at Jeanie who stood and watched. The bloodied woman wobbled over to the phone but Kristina got there first.

"No!" the teen girl said, ripping the phone off the hook.

Kristina would stab her aunt a total of five times in the back. There were also defensive wounds on her hand and lumps on her head.

Her aunt now dead, Kristina wanted a change of clothes. But first she rummaged through Arlene's bedroom, stealing her necklaces and other small pieces of jewelry.

"We need to find her damn keys," Kristina called out to Jeanie.

They searched for the keys to both the safe and the truck to no avail.

Kristina then thought she heard police sirens in the distance. The two girls began to run and Kristina started to cry.

The girls ran down the block, pounding on the doors of neighbors until police arrived.

"I killed my aunt," Kristina sobbed. "I killed my aunt."

"It was a grisly scene," Detective Neil Schwartz recalled as he came upon Arlene's body. "Brutal. Very bloody."

THE AFTERMATH

Kristina would be charged with first-degree murder and her case was transferred from the juvenile system to a district court in order for her to be tried as an adult.

Her defense team would enter a plea of insanity. She would undergo psychiatric examination with Dr. Michael Taylor who stated that he didn't think Kristina was insane but rather had a personality disorder.

Her planning was too precise and her deception upon entering her aunt's house did not suggest that she was insane, the doctor explained. Furthermore, she understood what she had done after the killing.

But another psychiatrist, Dr. Gaylord Nordine, believed that Kristina was in a psychotic state caused by the Prozac. Dr. Taylor disagreed, stating that Prozac would not have had any adverse consequences on her and that Kristina was also on Thorazine at the time which should have made more her even more docile.

"In talking with her I found absolutely no evidence of any type of psychiatric disorder, " Taylor said. "And in talking with her I found absolutely no indication that she was doing anything on October 25, 1994, other than killing her aunt."

On December 18th, 1995, Kristina would be sentenced to life in prison without parole.

She would serve out her sentence at the Iowa Correctional Institution for Women in Mitchellville, Iowa. She would file appeal after appeal as her attorneys would bring up the fact that this was cruel and unusual punishment for a juvenile.

According to her friends, Kristina didn't forgive herself for what she had done.

"When everybody else was telling her that they forgave her and they're showing her unconditional love," Jaimi Ross said. "She didn't feel she deserved it. It was very hard for her to accept."

Kristina and Jaimi would becoming close friends in jail. They had to...They were two children in an adult prison who were serving life sentences.

When other children came into the facility, Kristina and Jaimi would serve as mentors of sorts.

"They came in and everybody would share their story. It would be Kristina, myself, and another inmate. We'd just open ourselves up and let it all pour out and let them see us for the same flawed humans that they are."

A TERMINAL ILLNESS

In 2013, however, Kristina would be diagnosed with inoperable breast cancer. By November of that year, Kristina would be re-sentenced to life in prison with the possibility of parole.

The judge also recommended that she be immediately paroled due to her illness.

The decision on whether or not to set her free set off a firestorm of controversy in Kristina's own family and the state of Iowa.

"To give her her last few moments of joy and peace," Kristina's mother Denise Fetters said. "I think could be the best thing that she could receive."

But other family members weren't so keen on that idea.

"I just don't feel bad for Krissy for where she's at," Kristina's cousin, Shanna Sickles said. "She put herself there. She didn't give my Aunt Arlene the opportunity to die with her loved ones. Bottom line, if you get life in prison without the possibility of parole, it's life."

But Kristina also had her supporters in friend Jaimi Ross.

"I completely understand when people say things like 'Oh, a life for a life, she took a life, she should die in prison,'" Ross said. "That states more about where you're at in life, and not her, not me and not her family. I get that that's where your heart is and that's what you believe. Were not asking for her to have a second chance."

The parole board decided to release Kristina on a hospice-only basis. There was outcry from people who wanted her to stay in jail, stating that the prison only set her free to save on medical costs.

In the end, the bureaucracy mattered little as Kristina had already reached stage four with her cancer.

"No one can alter the past," Kristina's aunt Darcy Olson said. "It is what it is, this happened to our family and it's now time for my family to have closure. Kristina's impending death cannot be denied and while there have been negative comments, we believe, as the victims, our family has suffered enough and we ask the parole board to grant our request."

Darcy was the only family member aside from Kristina's mother that supported her during the trial and parole hearings.

"It's just so bitter sweet," Olson said. "This has been a 19-year old tragedy for my family. This will bring closure for my whole family and help us all cope just a little bit better with the situation."

"Everybody's like, well, she was a monster," Ross said. "She was evil. It would be so easy in this world if that were just the case. But that's not the way that it is. Not everybody that commits a crime...not everybody that's a sinner is evil or a monster. Her legacy, I hope, will challenge other people to see what they can do for kids. For teenagers. Before it gets to the point where they're in prison or needing to go before a judge for any reason."

The cancer would spread throughout her bones and spine. Kristina would live out her last days in pain.

"The screams I had to listen to last Sunday, no mother should ever have to hear in her life," Kristina's mother, Denise said.

Seven months into her release, Kristina would die at the age of thirty-four.

bonus:

Brittany Holberg was a twenty-three years old prostitute when she was convicted of murdering 80-year-old A.B. Towery Jr, stabbing him over sixty times.

The controversy surrounding the case centered around the relationship of Brittany and Towery prior to the killing. Brittany argued that Towery was a client who went into a rage when he found drugs on her person. He attacked her and she retaliated in self-defense.

Further investigation would reveal otherwise, however, as Brittany would use numerous household items in a brutal assault on the elderly man.

She fled the scene only to be caught at a McDonald's after police received a tip from a witness who saw her on "America's Most Wanted."

With her good looks and well-proportioned body, Brittany has remained in the spotlight as she was featured in a Maxim Magazine article as one of the "hottest women on death row".

Brittany still sits on death row today with her case being appealed on the numerous levels in the court system.

EARLY LIFE

Brittany was born on January 1, 1973, in Amarillo, Texas.

Accounts on Brittany's home life vary as she would manipulate according to the needs of her listener. To her probation officer, she informed them that her home life was "good" and that she "had everything that she ever wanted". She would often describe her mother as her best friend.

During other occasions, however, Brittany would paint a different story.

She would describe her parents as being "hippie-drugsters". Brittany would state that she was close to her mother but never knew her father, a heroin addict who was in and out of the Texas prison system. Her mother would later marry a man named John Schwartz with the couple marrying and divorcing four times.

They would drink heavily and openly smoke weed in front of the young Brittany who would be sexually assaulted by a babysitter at the age of five. When she was twelve, one of her aunts was murdered and according to Brittany "everything fell apart" at home. Her parents would leave her unattended as they indulged in pot and booze.

"They just stopped working," Brittany said. "They just let everything go."

She would be gang raped by two men who confronted her in an alley behind her home when she was thirteen.

Brittany would then spend the majority of her time living with her grandmother. By the age of sixteen, however, she would run away with her boyfriend Ward. The two would make it as far as California, get married, and have a young daughter named Mackenzie.

The union would not last long, however. Brittany would divorce Ward and move back to her native Amarillo. Ward would take Mackenzie and move to Tulsa, Oklahoma.

Brittany would state that she suffered a knee injury and would become addicted to pain medication during treatment. She would then graduate to harder drugs like cocaine.

In and out of rehab, Brittany's life spiraled out of control. She could manipulate with the best of them, however, and would escape from the Midland Halfway House with the help of a female counselor.

Brittany would hang out with the drug-using crowd and her own habits were out of control. To support her addiction, Brittany began working as a prostitute.

This would put her in harm's way on many an occasion as she would get gang-raped and beaten severely.

The assault would put her in the hospital but she would resume "tricking" when she was released.

"At that point in her life, Brittany was incorrigible," forensic psychologist Paula Orange said."Numerous people had reached to her and tried to help. She had extended family members trying to help.

Friends trying to help. Even church outreach workers. All to no avail. The drugs had taken root and she was dead set on manipulating everyone around her. Family, roommates, church members, doctors, dentists, and pharmacists would all fall victim to her schemes to get drugs."

By 1993, Brittany was a full-blown drug-addicted prostitute with the rap sheet to prove it. In April of that year, she would steal a gun from her step-father. She then passed over $1300 in "hot" checks and applied for several store credit cards using a fake name.

Brittany and one of her aunts would run a scam on dentists, lying to them about their pain levels in order to get prescription medication. When the prescription drugs ran out, she would return to street drugs like cocaine and heroin. Arrests would follow and Brittany would be charged in Hale County with drug possession, paraphernalia, and public intoxication.

Upon her release, Brittany would proceed to steal her mother's car and forge checks in her name. The prostitution continued unabated as well as she stole the wallet from one of her "tricks" who pressed charges.

While in jail for the theft, Brittany would be introduced to Ella Gibbs and Patricia Karnes who ran the ministry in the Randall County Jail. The women tried to get Brittany on the right track and introduce her to Christianity.

"I wanted to reassure Brittany that she is a valuable person, that her life has great potential, and that this is the mortal portion of an eternal life," Karnes said. " Brittany is an eternal being and through the many prayers from my [prayer] group [in Lubbock,] I have been led to come back into this child's life to support her here, to encourage her, to find her courage from the Holy Spirit within her, and to let her know that there is a human being mortal person who will stand beside her and see the good in her and support whatever God plans for the rest of your [sic] life."

A.B. TOWERY

Towery was by all accounts a nice man. His son would bristle at the idea that he was Brittany's "sugar daddy".

"Dad wasn't a dirty old man," his son said. "Dad was just trying to help somebody and look what he got, and now she's getting three meals a day and a warm place to sleep."

The defense would later bring up the fact that he once pulled a knife on his son Russell during a temper tantrum. Towery would have a history with prostitutes (according to court testimony). Connie Baker would be a prostitute from the 1980s to 1997 and stated that Towery was one of her clients. Baker would also claim Tower as a client but she also had a history of drug possession and auto theft. Diana Wheeler would also admit to being one of Towery's prostitutes in the years of 1994 and 1995. She had come to his home and he even went so far as to clean the stains off his Mel Mac dinnerware. But Wheeler also had a long criminal history like Baker, arrested for prostitution, criminal trespass and giving false identification to a police officer.

The controversy at the trial was if Brittany and Towery had an ongoing "sex-for-money" relationship.

This would be vigorously discounted by family members.

His daughter-in-law would come to the home and help with some housekeeping. His sons would also visit daily and never report any "ladies of the evening" coming to visit their father.

The picture just didn't fit.

Brittany stated she was sent to Towery's place by a fellow streetwalker who went by the moniker of "Green Eyes" but that it was later revealed that no such prostitute by that name existed. Brittany had lied like she had so many times before.

The two seemed to have met by chance.

COMING BACK FROM THE GROCERY STORE

November 13th, 1996 was another normal day for the 80-year old A.B Towery. He had just purchased groceries at an Albertson's store and was walking back to his apartment. As he entered the courtyard, he was approached by the 23-year old Brittany Holberg.

She asked to use his telephone and Towery consented. He wanted to help the sweet-voiced Brittany and didn't believe that she posed any kind of physical threat to him.

What he didn't know was that Brittany was coming down from a cocaine high and had not slept in ten days.

"Brittany could be persuasive," Orange said. "She was well-versed in how to charm people, she knew exactly what to say and do in terms of body language. She was like a trained actress. It didn't take much cajoling on her part to convince Towery to let her inside his home. He probably thought 'what's the big deal?'"

Once inside, Brittany would demand money from the elderly man but he refused. Brittany then attacked Towery, trying to strong arm the wallet out of his pocket. The struggle began in the living room. The two then pushed and pulled each other around a partition that separated the kitchen from the living room. They then returned to the living room. At some point, Towery tried to leave the apartment but Brittany pulled him back in. The evidence also indicated that the two paused during this 45-minute fight, catching their breath and nursing their wounds. Brittany would sustain minor stab wounds to her stomach and thigh.

"This was most likely a fight that had a lot of clutching and grabbing," Orange said. "There was less blood in the living room so the conjecture is that is where the fight started. There was blood near the door so that suggests that Towery was bleeding out and trying to escape for help. Remember, he was a slow-moving 80-year old man. Brittany was a young woman but she was fueled by cocaine. He's getting tired a lot faster than she will."

Eventually, Brittany gained the upper hand. She used various objects around the home to beat down Towery. She started with a cast iron frying pan, then a steam iron, a claw hammer, a fruit knife, a butcher knife and then two forks. Towery would fall to the floor, a bloody mess.

Brittany then took a lamp and shoved its base five inches down his throat which choked him to death.

Satisfied that he had finally killed Tower, Brittany removed her bloody clothes. She washed up in his bathroom then went to his closet to find some clothes that fit her.

Walking back to his dead body, Brittany retrieved the wallet out of Towery's pocket. She took out the $1400 dollars he had and dropped the now empty wallet onto his stomach.

Brittany casually walked out of the apartment and hitched a ride with a young couple. The couple dropped her off at a local crack house where Brittany paid them off with two $100 bills (which had blood stains on them). Inside the drug den, Brittany befriended the proprietor and changed clothes again. She then went to a local hotel with hundreds of dollars worth of cocaine and indulged.

TRIAL

Brittany's defense attorney, Catherine Brown Dodson, would argue that Holberg acted in self-defense when she killed Towery. Her primary argument was that Towery was far from an innocent, elderly man. He was, in fact, a drug abuser himself who became physically violent with Brittany when he found a crack pipe on her person. He then hit Brittany two times in the head when she turned her back to him. Brittany retaliated and ultimately put the lamp post in his mouth in an attempt to end the fight.

Brittany then fled as she believed that no one would believe her side of the story because she was both a prostitute and a drug addict.

While in jail, Brittany would try to coerce Katina Dixon, her cellmate to kill Vickie Marie Kirkpatrick who was the prosecution witness.

Towery's history with prostitutes would be brought up in court testimony. They would also mention incidents of violence with his ex-wife and children but jurors didn't believe the old man was in any type of shape to employ the service of a prostitute.

"My father didn't even like the word 'sex'", one of his sons said. "He was old-fashioned."

A psychiatrist would testify, however, that Brittany had battered wife syndrome, post-traumatic stress disorder, and cocaine addiction.

The jury did not take long to deliberate, finding Brittany to be a cunning, manipulative liar who committed one of the most brutal crimes in the history of Amarillo.

They would find her guilty and Brittany would be moved to death row at Gatesville, Texas.

"I can't even explain to you," Brittany said in a magazine interview. "What it's like to have someone say 'You are sentenced to die.' It's words. You feel helpless, numb. It's almost as if your emotions shut you down."

Brittany would spend her first few weeks in prison laying prone on her bed in a zombie-like state. Over time, she grew accepting of her situation. She knew she was going to die but made it a point to learn to take each day one step at a time.

Her inspiration for cleaning up her act came from the memory of her daughter Mackenzie.

"I cannot live," Brittany said. "And I cannot die, knowing that my child has to live with the horror that these people tried to say about me, the story of the crime, their depiction that I was a cold-blooded person."

Brittany states that she dedicates her days to reading, writing to family and working on her law appeals. She also is anti-death penalty advocate.

She would follow other Texas inmates who were now on death row and make appeals on their behalf, specifically that of Betty Lou Beets.

"I realized," Brittany said. "It doesn't matter whether I'm guilty or innocent, this has now become a very political thing... At this point, they're just killing to kill."

She complained that after a recent jail uprising, the treatment of death row inmates has worsened.

"You would not believe the treatment we are given," Brittany said. "Just two weeks ago, we were informed that not only would we be strip-searched for our one hour of recreation a day, but also when taken for a shower. So for the last two weeks, we have been stripped no less than six times a day. This is every day, sometimes at times like 2:30-3 a.m., and we never leave the building or our cells for that matter."

As of this writing, Brittany's stay of execution has been appealed and appealed for the past eighteen years.

Her attorneys would exhaust the appeal process in the state system but it is now in the federal courts.

Her case, however, has been costing taxpayers "conservatively to be at least $400,000" according to county criminal attorney James Farren. In the future, he has decided to forgo seeking the death penalty in capital cases.

Farren continues to favor a death penalty but only under certain circumstances like "a guy walks into a day care center and kills the children or if someone kills a police officer or a firefighter in the line of duty."

Farren predicted that Brittany would remain on death row for another five years at least. "They can go through the U.S District Court in Amarillo, then it can go to the Fifth U.S Circuit Court and the U.S. Supreme Court. Then from there it can go back to the U.S. District."

But the appeals can come to a halt if the district judge refuses to hear it again.

"If the Supreme Court says 'no," Farren said. "That's when the district judge can feel safe in stopping this process."

The entire process has been an infuriating one for the Towery family. His son both rages and mourns about what happened to his father.

"She tried to apologize to us during the trial," Russel Towery said. " I got up and walked out. I'm sure other families are going through the same things I'm going through. It's been almost 19 years ... people forget."

"I don't want to die before she does. I want to stand there as she's kicking and screaming going to the death gurney. I want her to think about what my dad went through when she didn't even know his name," he said. "She thinks that because she said she was sorry, that everything's all right. ... she is evil and needs to be destroyed."

KILLER TEEN NIKKI REYNOLDS

SAMANTHA REED

It is not often that stories appear where we find the perpetrators of violence being children and the victims being parents. Although, scattered throughout history it has been seen that children can be capable of shocking amounts of violence, and many, assuming their innocent nature, fall victim to them. In Coral Springs, Florida in 1997 one such story took place. And still the actions of the evening resonate throughout the community.

In The Beginning

Born in 1979 to a mother that didn't want her, Jacquiline "Nikki" Reynolds was adopted by Robert and Billie Jean Reynolds three months after her birth. The Reynolds were a loving, Christian family from Coral Springs, Florida and they were delighted to welcome their new daughter into their lives.

There was nothing that they wouldn't do for Nikki. Robert Reynolds worked for the Department of Transportation and Billie Jean was an administrative assistant at RJ Reynolds. They had a quiet home and they were devoted to making their daughter happy.

Nikki was a good child. She was devoted to the church, like her parents, and she loved her parents deeply. She would go to the mall with her mother or watch baseball games with her father. She could never spend too much time with them. The Reynolds did everything to ensure that Nikki was being raised in a loving and non-judgmental environment.

Friends and family would agree that the environment was loving, but the Reynolds gave Nikki everything she wanted. She was pampered, she was spoiled, and in the end, she was a bit of a brat. Sometimes the best intentions can have the worst consequences.

Still, Nikki, as she got older, became a good student and didn't act out. She achieved good grades in school and went out of her way to become involved in extra curricular activities. She also stayed heavily involved with the church alongside her parents.

By all appearances, Nikki was the perfect child. She was the child that most parents dream of having and Robert and Billie Jean were delighted with her. But children grow up, despite anything that their parents try to do to stop it, and Nikki was no exception. And not all children grow up in a manner that their parents can be proud of.

The Beginning of the End

Nikki went from being the model child to what most people would call a 'troubled teen'. It didn't start in the way one would expect, with failing grades and a lack of interest in school. It started with a lie, and one that shocked family and friends in the disturbing nature of it.

In 1996, sixteen-year-old Nikki came home from school and claimed that she had been assaulted after getting off of the school bus. Naturally her parents were shocked and appalled to hear that this had happened to her. They immediately called the police to handle the situation officially. Nikki claimed she had been attacked by someone she knew, at first. But when questioned by the police her story quickly changed.

She went on to say that she didn't know her attacker and then that the attack hadn't happened at all. She hadn't been raped. She'd made the whole story up.

Now why would a sixteen-year-old, devote Christian girl make up a story about being raped? Why would she go to the extreme of telling her parents and getting the police involved if it was just a story?

It turns out that Nikki hadn't been raped. Rather she was in a relationship, the first one of a sexual nature in her lifetime, and she was terrified to tell her parents about it. She was worried about what they would think about their daughter sacrificing her morals and her principles just to have a boyfriend. But Carlos Infante was her entire world. The sixteen-year-old classmate was consuming her life focus to the point that she hadn't hesitated to throw caution to the wind.

And when the thought of telling her parents about what was going on had come up, in her mind, fabricating a rape story had seemed like a better idea. Nikki was also concerned that she might be pregnant, a worry that was quickly put to rest, but it also influenced her decision to pursue the rape narrative.

Billie Jean was extremely unhappy with Nikki, potentially for the first time during her parenting of the girl. She didn't like the fact that Nikki had a boyfriend. She didn't like the fact that she'd sacrificed her principles and morals, the beliefs that they thought they'd instilled into her all for some boy. They believed that they'd raised a good, Christian girl and for the first time they were starting to question that belief.

Bille Jean and Robert disliked the idea of Nikki having a boyfriend, it didn't particularly matter who he was. They viewed it as a step down for her. They saw it as a complete abandonment of her belief system, something they had strived to instill in her over the course of her entire life. She was sacrificing everything in order to be with this boy, from their point of view. She was losing herself in him. And Billie Jean and Robert wanted to help get Nikki back on a clear path, on a Christian path.

So, they insisted that she spend less time with Carlos and more time with the church. They hoped that in doing so she would see her wrongdoings and find her true self again. They hoped that in spending more time with the church that she would become closer to the family again and forget about Carlos.

Billie Jean believed that Nikki needed to spend more time with a better group of people, a Christian group of people. She hoped that if Nikki spent time around other good, Christian kids that she would find her way again, that she would find a better crowd. And Billie Jean was willing to go to great lengths to ensure that her daughter found a path that fit with the beliefs and morals of the family.

But sometimes the child, no matter how much they push, cannot realize the hopes and dreams of parents. And sometimes, despite all efforts, things still go wrong.

Rebellion Continues

Teenage rebellion can be a strong force, however, and the more that Billie Jean pushed Nikki to go to church the more she resisted. Nikki said, "I knew that the way I was living was not right in God's eyes, but I did not want to hear all of that." She was too engulfed in her life with Carlos. He was quickly becoming her entire world and nothing else mattered to her. Not her parents, and certainly not her church.

The rebellion was extending into her school life. Nikki, who had once been a good student with marks that her parents could be proud of was now beginning to skip class. Her grades were beginning to fall as a result and she was no longer the academic force that she was before.

It was to the point that Billie Jean and Robert barely recognized the girl that they had raised anymore. Who was this young woman living in their house? She reflected none of the morals and principles they had raised her to uphold. She wouldn't listen to them. She opposed them at every turn. They began to wonder what had happened to their daughter Nikki. Where had she gone?

Nikki went from a happy-go-lucky child that was a pleasure to be around, a child who was soft spoken and loved to go to church to a girl no one could recognize. She wore dark clothes, she changed her music, she changed her bedroom to dark colours – she became the opposite of herself. It was hard to tell if this was simply teenage rebellion or something more going on. Was this all because of Carlos or was there some deeper problem at play?

She slept a lot, more than any teenager should and she isolated herself from her family. Gone were the days of ice cream and base ball games. She no longer went on trips to the mall with her mother. She no longer went to church with her family. She became disinterested in many things that used to hold her attention, things that used to captivate her. Her whole world now revolved around Carlos.

It was her first sexual relationship with anyone in her life and it had reached the point of obsession. She filled her diary with everything to do with Carlos. Her room was plastered with photos of him. Her every waking moment revolved around him. There was an unnatural intensity to her emotions towards him, an unhealthy intensity. And it was quickly becoming evident that this was a problem.

Naturally, Billie Jean and Robert were very concerned about their daughter's current mental state. She was not herself, and the only thing they could blame was Carlos as he was the only changing factor in her life. It seemed that he was a negative influence on Nikki in many ways. He didn't make good grades as a student, and now her grades were plummeting as well.

Billie Jean was also worried that he was coming over every day, potentially when they were at work. They had no way to confirm this, but she didn't like the idea that he was at the house alone with her while they were at work. It didn't sit well with her.

So Billie Jean put her foot down, perhaps for the first time in her experience as a parent. She began to tell Nikki no, especially when it came to Carlos. And Nikki handled it with the maturity level of a toddler as opposed to that of a teenager. Nikki threw awful tantrums. Billie Jean and Nikki would engage in screaming matches in the house that would result in slammed doors. The result was very wearing on Billie Jean. She found herself screaming at Nikki almost all of the time. This was not what she wanted her life as a mother to be. This was not the girl she had raised. She needed to do something about this, but she was at a loss as to what the solution could be.

And despite the screaming matches and the orders to stay away, Nikki still kept seeing Carlos. It seemed that nothing could keep her from Carlos. She would sneak out at night when everyone was asleep to see him and it didn't matter what the consequences were.

Billie Jean's frustration escalated to the point that one day she confided in a friend saying "Don't be surprised if one day you come home and there's police cars and fire trucks up and down the street 'cause one of us, it'll be me or Nikki, but one of us will be gone."

Billie Jean's prediction would prove to hit a little too close to home in the coming days. And the aftermath would shock everyone.

Intervention

It was May 14, 1997 when the school counselor contacted Billie Jean to tell her that there was trouble with Nikki and Carlos. She asked that Billie Jean come in and speak with her in person and that Billie Jean, Robert, and Nikki come in for a full meeting the next day. Upon visiting the high school, the counselor told Billie Jean that Nikki and Carlos had more than just the usual high school relationship issues to deal with.

That day Nikki had told the counselor that she was pregnant with Carlos' baby. This had naturally prompted the counselor to contact Billie Jean immediately about the issue. Billie Jean, having already dealt with Nikki's questionable honesty with the previous rape accusation, was hesitant to believe the pregnancy claim. She was fairly certain that this was another one of Nikki's schemes, but there was a sure way to determine its legitimacy.

So she took Nikki to the drug store to find out what was what.

The results of the pregnancy test were negative. That didn't mean Billie Jean was any less pleased with her daughter. Nikki called Carlos with the news. And despite having a counseling meeting the next day Billie Jean decided to seek guidance from a higher power. She dragged Nikki away from the phone and took Nikki to see the church counselor.

Nikki spoke with her pastor as they waited to see the counselor. He was supportive as he talked to her about her boyfriend problems and offered her guidance. Their conversation with the counselor did not have the same supportive tone. The counselor spent the session telling Nikki that her mother did not deserve the behaviour she was displaying. She raised her voice and yelled at Nikki. This didn't go over very well.

Nikki removed herself from the office and from the church. She wanted nothing more to do with the impromptu counseling session. And as she stood in the parking lot of the church she even debated removing herself from the family by running away. But she didn't run away, however. Instead, she took a higher ground, something that hadn't been seen from her in almost a year. She went back into the counselor's office and apologized to her mother. And she finished the session with the counselor before returning home with her mother.

Billie Jean believed that they had made a step in the right direction. She would be the one to learn how wrong she was about that fact.

Confusion and Confessions

It was barely an hour after their visit to the counselor on May 14, 1997 that the call came in to 911. At 7:07pm Nikki Reynolds' panicked voice came over the phone saying "I stabbed her repeatedly in the back. There's blood all over her and all over the floor and everything."

Police were at her house in minutes and the scene that they witnessed was one that would stay with some of the officers for years after. When police arrived they found Nikki waiting on her doorstep. One of the officers who responded indicated that "She had blood all over, blood on her legs, blood on her face."

Nikki was placed in the back of the police car and left to wait while the police went to investigate. A tape recorder was left on with her in the police car so that anything that was said while she was alone was recorded and on file. It recorded her praying that her mother was still be alive and saying that she had learned her lesson. She was asking God to forgive her and for her mother to please still be alive.

Her mother was brought out of the house on a stretcher by the EMTs and she was still alive at the time that she left the house. However, Billie Jean was pronounced dead at the hospital at 8:10pm after suffering from 13 stab wounds.

Nikki was taken to the police department immediately. Robert came home from work to find the house in a state of chaos, surrounded by police cars and police tape. He hadn't yet been informed of the situation that had come to pass behind the front doors of his home. He broke down at the news that his wife was gone and that his daughter was responsible. The shock of it was something that he couldn't quite comprehend.

The scene inside the house was gruesome and shocking to police investigators. It depicted Billie Jean's terrible, drawn out death as she fought to get away from her daughter. But there was no escape for her as she was stabbed repeatedly until she finally lay immobile on the floor.

The police found the kitchen knife that had been used as the murder weapon in the sink and it still had blood on it. They also found evidence that someone, likely Nikki, had attempted to clean up the scene using towels and dishcloths. The blood soaked pieces of cloth were scattered about the kitchen unable to handle the sheer amount of blood that had resulted from the incident.

While the police officers worked diligently at the crime seen the detectives questioned Nikki about the murder. And it didn't take too much effort to get her to talk.

"I didn't have any intentions of lying." Nikki said. "I didn't have any secrets. I wanted to get it out." She felt almost compelled to tell the story of what had happened. She needed to let them know.

"It was simple, all I had to ask her was what happened today and just started chatting. She went through the whole story from a to b," said the detective who interviewed Nikki.

The story that was told by Nikki revolved heavily around Carlos Infante, the infamous boyfriend. Nikki had used her fake pregnancy to keep Carlos in a relationship with her when he wanted to leave, fearing what would happen if he left. When she had found out she was not pregnant, for sure, she called him to give the news. Carlos indicated that he wanted nothing to do with her and all of her lies. He'd had enough. Billie Jean had even got on the phone with Carlos and apologized for all of the drama that he'd had to endure at the hands of her daughter.

Nikki had decided then and there that someone would die that day. She even took a handful of aspirin before going to the counseling meeting with her mother at the church. She was certain that she could overdose on it. She was certain that it would be her that would die.

However, when the overdose failed her thoughts went from suicide to homicide rather quickly. But the intended victim had not been her mother.

Her plan had been to get a hold of Carlos the next day and kill him. She figured she could catch him after first hour and slash his throat if she snuck up behind him. She believed that if she couldn't have him then no one should be allowed to have him. He belonged to her essentially.

However, the one obstacle in her plan to kill Carlos was the meeting they had with the guidance counselor the next day. Nikki was unsure whether she would be sent home after the meeting or not. In order to kill Carlos she would have to skip the guidance meeting. So, in order to accomplish this, she figured she would have to kill her parents as well. She would just wait until they were sleeping and then simply slash their throats. Then they could no longer stand in her way.

A real obstacle came into this metaphorical plan when her father left for church after dinner that night alone and her mother stayed home. This was very out of character for them. Nikki also stayed home as her mother told her she was grounded for the rest of the evening. She was instructed to clean the dishes after dinner.

Nikki decided that she would just roll with this change. She believed, since she was now home alone with her mother, that it would be much easier to kill her mother now, clean up the mess, and then wait until her father returned. She could then kill him and do the same. Finally, she could drive herself to school in the morning, wait for

Carlos, and kill him after first hour just like she had planned. It would work out perfectly.

Logical thought was gone at this point in time. Nikki was acting strictly on whatever thoughts came to her mind and they were frantic, desperate. Still, she waited for her opportunity to arrive. She waited for her moment when she could kill her mother.

Opportunity came while she was cleaning up in the kitchen and Billie Jean was working at her computer. Nikki took a kitchen knife, paused for a moment to check the blade for its sharpness, and then slowly approached her mother. She hesitated now that she had the knife in hand. She wasn't sure what it would feel like to slash someone's throat.

When she finally got up the nerve to come up behind her mother and attempt to cut her throat it didn't slash it, it only cut it. Billie Jean jumped up in surprise and darted towards the laundry room. She screamed, "No, Nikki, no."

"I told her I had to kill her because I can't live without Carlos," Nikki explained to police in her interview.

Nikki kept stabbing her because she wanted to put her out of her misery, she claims. She didn't want her mother to suffering any longer. And in her last moments, Billie Jean still offered her daughter forgiveness for killing her.

Nikki spent one night in the hospital because of her claim of ingesting a large amount of Aspirin. After that she was turned over to the county jail where she was formally booked on a charge of First Degree Murder.

The First Trial

The first trial for Nikki Reynolds lasted from April 14, 1999 – May 3, 1999.

If convicted, Nikki faced life in prison after spending two years in a Juvenile Detention Centre. The prosecution built their case around Nikki's obsession with Carlos Infante, making sure to indicate that he was not at fault in any way and rather he was also one of the three listed on Nikki's kill list.

The defence opted to take an insanity plea route, rather than try to dispute the charge that Nikki had committed the murder – something she had confessed to multiple times. This defence fell flat. The criterion for an insanity plea is very strict. The accused has to suffer from a serious mental illness and the accused has to be unaware that what they are doing is wrong or has consequences.

The psychologist that testified for the prosecution indicated that Nikki was well aware of what she was doing, and rather that she was just a confused girl. The defence tried to argue that Nikki suffered from Borderline Personality disorder. They claimed that individuals suffering from this disorder could idolize the individuals they are with and then suddenly snap, and become violent. Which is very similar to Nikki's reaction after Carlos indicated he wanted nothing to do with her. They also claimed that the Aspirin played a part as Aspirin can cause metabolic imbalances and psychosis upon overdoes.

Regardless of the claims on either side, the jury was hung and the trial ended in a mistrial.

The Second Trial

Second trail for Nikki Reynolds began on Sept 1, 1999.

Similar to the first, the prosecution brought a series of psychologists to the stand to prove that, while not a rational act, Nikki was not insane. The prosecution also claimed that her mother's death was premeditated.

The defence countered that Nikki was mentally ill and called experts to speak to Nikki's sanity. The defence also brought forward Nikki's biological mother to testify. The birth mother had a long history of mental illness and family violence. The defence argued that it was the anxiety over losing Carlos that pushed Nikki over the edge and brought her mental illness to the surface.

After much deliberation, Nikki Reynolds was found guilty of Second Degree Murder at the end of the trial.

At the sentencing hearing on January 7, 2000 Nikki's biological mother made a plea to include treatment as a part of Nikki's sentence. She believed that her daughter needed help, much like she had needed help in her lifetime.

Nikki also addressed the court, pleading with the judge to sentence her to a psychiatric facility instead of prison. She truly believed that there had been something wrong that day, if not insanity, than something else. She believed that she needed help. She bore no ill will towards her family. She hated none of them. She had never hated them and still didn't.

However, the judge believed that the wrongness of what she had done to outweigh all else. He gave her the maximum sentence under Florida law, 34 years in prison. She was resentenced to 21 years and 8 months on April 4, 2001 due to a change in sentencing laws in the state of Florida.

In the end Robert Reynolds remarried in 1998 and has had no contact with his daughter since she was sent to prison on January 2000.

And Nikki was incarcerated at the Gadsden Correctional Facility in Quincy, Florida. She was eligible for parole in 2015 and was released.